Profitable Technical Analysis

3rd Edition

Tony Pow

Contents

Highlights 5
   The power of market timing 6
   How to beat the S&P 500 index by 100% 9
   Bubbles 10
Introduction 12
      Disclaimer 16
      How the rate of return is calculated 16
Section I: Technical Analysis (TA) 17
   Overview of Technical Analysis 18
   1   Technical analysis (TA) 20
   2   Examples of using TA 25
   3   Easy TA without charts 28
   4   More on technical analysis 29
   5   Using Finviz.com as a screener example 30
   6   Finviz's parameters 32
      Your broker's website 39
      Other sources 40
      Gurus 41
      Quick and dirty 41
      5-minute stock evaluation 42
   7   Using Fidelity 43
   8   Bollinger Bands 44
   9   MACD 45
   10   Double Tops 45
   11   Other TA indicators/patterns 49
   12   Peaking and Overbought 50
   13   Using SMA-20 & SMA-50 on stocks 51
   14   Using TA for sectors 54
   15   Fundamentals vs. Charts 57

16	Momentum and volatility	60
17	How to determine a reversal	61
18	Determine the exit point	62
19	Volume	64
20	A TA strategy	64

Bonus: Market Timing 65

1	Market timing example	66
	Management summary	66
	Mid-year update	71
	Canary warning?	73
	A correction or a crash?	74
2	Simplest market timing	75
3	Why the market fluctuates	79
4	Market cycle	81
5	Market timing by calendar	88
6	Profitable Early Recovery	92
7	Market timing of 2022	94

Epilogue 96

Appendix 1 – All my books 97

Best stocks to buy for 2025 102
Art of Investing 103

Appendix 2: Reviews by the unbiased AI 108

Review of "Art of Investing 5th Edition " 9/10 108
  ChatGPT Review 108
  DeepSeek Review 109
Review of " Best stocks to buy for 2025" 113
Review of "Sector Rotation 5th Edition" rated 9.5 115
Review of "Your first dollar for smart investing " 117
  ChatGPT 117

Final Thoughts from DeepSeek: 118
Review of "Momentum Investing 3rd Edition " 119
Review of "Using profitable investment sites" rated 8 120
Review of "Investing successes and blunders" 121
Appendix 3 - Our window to the investing world 123
Appendix 4 - ETFs / Mutual Funds 123
Appendix 5 - Links 129

Highlights

My motivation to write this book

I would like to share my experiences, both good and bad. I use simple-to-follow techniques using the free (or low-cost) resources available to us. I have been successful in investing for decades. I am enjoying a comfortable financial life. I do not hold back my 'secrets' as my children are not interested in investing. I offer you a small legacy in sharing my investing ideas.

If you are looking at how to make a 100% return overnight, there are many other books claiming to do so, and then this book is not for you. This book describes how to be a 'turtle' investor making a fortune gradually and surely. Before you begin, first define your objectives.

My steps to trade stocks (ETFs are far simpler)

1. Search for valued stocks (there are many strategies to choose from).
2. Evaluate the screened stocks by
    a. Fundamental Analysis.
    b. Intangible Analysis.
    c. Qualitative Analysis.
    d. Technical Analysis.
3. Sell stocks.
   Every 6 months (shorter duration for some strategies), perform the same as in Step #2 to determine whether you need to sell the stocks you own, or just keep them for another 6 months.

The power of market timing

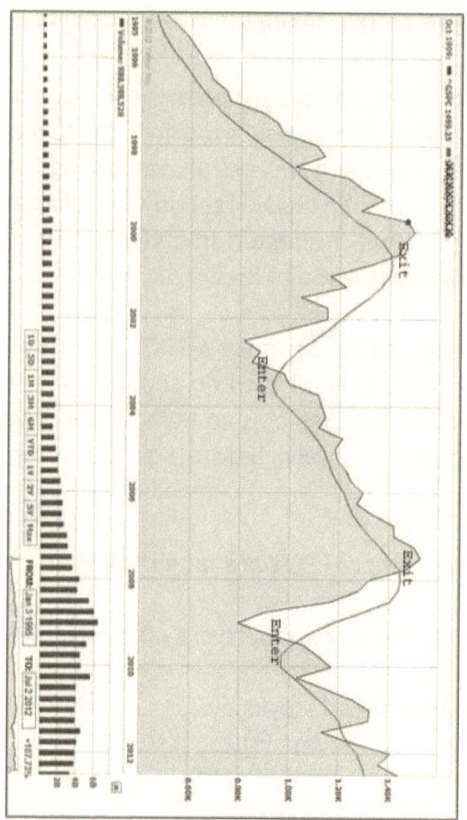

Most e-book readers allow you to select the graph to make it fit entirely on your screen. I use SPY, an ETF simulating the market. Detecting market plunges as seen in this graph indicates the exit points and reentry points also from 2000 to 9-2009 as follows.

Market Plunge	Peak	Bottom	Indicator Exit	Indicator Reenter
2000	08/28/00	09/20/02	10/01/00	06/01/03
2007	10/12/07	03/06/09	02/01/08	09/01/09
			08/01/11	11/01/11

Table: Vital Dates

For simplicity I skipped a few brief exits and reentries since 2011. You can run the simple chart once a month. When it indicates a potential market plunge is close, run the chart once a week. The last row represents a false signal.

This is based on stock prices so it may not identify the peaks and bottoms precisely, but so far it has not failed to avoid big losses and ensure big gains by reentering the market. I hope the next market plunge will most likely give us enough time to act as these two did.

Unbelievable return with market timing
Calculate how much you made if you followed the above exit points and reenter points from 2000 to today. I bet you would have made a good fortune.

I compared the above returns with the SPY without market timing from 1-2000 to 9-2013.

There are many assumptions. Dividends and compounding are not considered. My return should be substantially better if I include buying contra ETFs during the exits and selling them during the reentries. I was shocked by the incredible return by using this simple market timing. Again, past performance does not guarantee future performances.

Summary info:

S&P 500 1-2000 to 9-2013	With Market Timing	Without Market Timing
Better	**500%**	
Gain	1,000	167
Gain %	68%	11%
Annualized gained	5%	1%
Days	4,959	4,959

Calculations:

S & P 500	With Market Timing	Without Market Timing
1-2000	1,469[1]	1,469[1]
Exit 10/01/00	1,041[2]	1,041
Enter 06/01/03	1,041	964[4]
Exit 02/01/08	1,489[3]	1,379[4]
Enter 09/01/09	1489	1,020[5]
Exit 08/01/11	1,888	1,293
Enter 11/01/11	1,888	1,251
09/03/13	2,469	1.638
Gained	2,469 – 1,469=1,000	1,638-1,469=167

Gain %	1000/1469 = 68%	167/1469 = 11%
Annualized gained	68% * 365/4959=5%	11%*365/4959=1%
Better	(1,000-167)/167 = 500%	

Portfolio with Market Timing:
[1] Both start with S&P 500 of 1,469 on 1-3-2000.
[2] 10/01/00
The market timing portfolio exits the market and remains the same value of 1,041 until 6/1/00.
[3] 02/01/08
The market timing portfolio exits the market and remains the same value of 1,489 until 9/1/09.

'1,489' is calculated as follows:
1,041 * (1 + Rate) = 1,041 * (1 + 1,379-964)/964) = 1,489
where the S&P 500 is 964 on 6/1/00 and 1,379 on 2/1/08.

The other calculations are based on the S&P 500 at 1,020 on 9/1/9, 1,293 on 8/1/11, 1,251 on 11/1/11 and 1,636 on 9/3/13.

Portfolio without Market Timing:
[1] Both starts with the S&P 500 of 1,469 on 1-3-2000. We could use the 9/3/13 the S&P 500 value, but it would not account for some compounded interest considerations.

[4] S&P 500 is 964 on 6/1/00 and 1,379 on 2/1/08.

[5] 02/01/08. The portfolio value is calculated to be 1,020 as follows:
1,379 * (1 + Rate) = 1,379 * (1 + (1020-1379)/1379) = 1,020
where S&P 500 is 1,379 on 2/1/08 and 1,020 on 9/1/09.

The other calculations are based on the S&P 500 at 1,293 on 8/1/11, 1,251 on 11/1/11 and 1,636 on 9/3/13.

I cannot believe the shocking return with market timing. I checked my calculations and there was nothing wrong that I could find. If you find something wrong, send your findings to me (pow_tony@yahoo.com).

Even if I made a mistake somehow and got 100% instead of 500%, it still doubles the return without market timing! Ask any fund manager what it means to his or her fund performance and his / her career.

My simple technique that does not use chart told us to **exit the market** on around March 20, 2022.

How to beat the S&P 500 index by 100%

I recommended 20 stocks in an article Amazing Return in Seeking Alpha, a website for investors. If you bought them on the published date and then you would have beaten the S&P 500 index by over 100% without considering dividends as demonstrated in my other article A Tale of Two Portfolios. One of the many techniques is my Pow P/E as illustrated in another article The Mysteries of P/E.

Let's say I made a mistake and it is only a 10% gain. How many fund managers can beat the S&P 500 index by 10% regularly?

Filler

I got a call from Buffett asking me to lead their stock research.
I asked him why for nobody such as myself. No kidding.

He told me that he should have read my book Scoring Stocks to buy Apple instead of IBM in May, 2013. It would save his company millions of dollars minus $10 for my book. Not to mention the market timing technique that had worked in the last two major market plunges.

I told him, "OK, I'll beat your mediocre returns of the last 5 years."
He said, "You can do better than that and at least beat SPY. If you do so, no one will be that stupid to leave my fund and pay the hefty capital gain taxes."

I told him, "I cannot beat the market as you are the market especially after your expensive fees. In addition, I do not know how to avoid day traders from riding my wagon in trading. Also most of my big profits were made in small stocks that your fund cannot trade besides owning the company."

I woke up trembling. I'm glad it is only a nightmare.

Bubbles

Bubbles have existed throughout our history. Bubbles occur due to the excessive valuation most likely driven up by the big institutional investors (fund managers, pension managers, hedge fund manager, etc.). Asset valuations are then driven even higher by the retail investors. For example in 3/2014, the market bubble was caused by the government stimulus with the injection of capital into the excessive money supply and subsidies. The first investors riding the wave made good money, and the last ones buying at the peak will lose.

From our recent history, we have the 2000 internet bubble, and then the 2007 (2008 for some) housing bubble. The chapter "Spotting Big Market Plunges" illustrates it was easy to detect the last two plunges. It could save us more than 25% of your portfolio in the next plunge.

Today most of the mentioned bubbles could be caused by pumping too much money into the economy by the government. However, the government cannot keep on injecting money into the economy, and ask our children to pay for our debts forever. When the injections stop, the market will drop fast and deep.

USD

As of mid-2020, the USD is doing quite well. It could be the other countries (EU and Japan) are doing worse than us, as Einstein said, "everything is relative". The strong USD is not good for exports and the global corporations would have less profits after converting them back to USD. However, the excessive printing and high government debts would shake the status of USD as a reserve currency. It will also be hurt if China sells the U.S. Treasury bonds she owns.

Bond

The bond bubble will burst when the interest rates rise. Also it will as the interest rates should have been bottomed by as of mid-2020. It is possible that it could go negative.

Stocks

There are several bubble stocks such as FAANGs. The market was peaking in Jan., 2020 before the virus breakout. Play defense with stop loss orders. The record of margin debt is a big concern. When the credit is tightened with higher interest rate, this bubble will burst.

When to act

Without a time machine, no one can pinpoint when most of these bubbles will burst. Your timing to act depends on your risk tolerance, your knowledge and your greed.

Today, we have the housing bubble (2007-2008), the gold bubble, the market bubble, the second housing bubble, the debt bubble, the bond bubble, the second market bubble, etc. It seems like we can never get out of the bubble cycle. In 2020, the world would be in a global recession if the trade war between the two largest economies continue. It would be worse if the trade war turns into a military war.

Since the world is economically connected better than before. When the U.S.A. sneezes, it affects our trading partners such as European countries along with China and Japan, and also their partners such as the resource-rich countries of S. America, Australia, Russia, Canada and Africa.

For me, it is safer not to try to make the last buck when the reward / risk ratio is too low. A good sleep would improve your health which is worth all the gold in the world.

Introduction

This book describes the practical and useful technical indicators to predict the stock market (emphasized), sectors and stocks. Technical analysis is the most effective way to time the market followed by timing the sectors.

It is less effective to time the stocks as it depends on many other factors. However, many fundamental metrics do not include new products, new drugs and/or better earnings. When insiders and/or the institutional investors are buying, it will be detected by technical analysis.

Many technical indicators are damaging if they're not properly used. Prefer to master some of the practical and useful ones.

No one including all the Federal Reserve chairman and all the Nobel-Prize winners in economics can predict market plunges. Many predicted correctly market crashes by pure luck and some even received Nobel Prizes and became famous.

There is no model and formula to predict market plunges except my simple chart described in this book. It works for the last two market plunges and hopefully it will work to the next market plunge.

The chart depends on the falling stock prices, so it will not detect the bottoms and peaks precisely, but it will prevent further losses and reenter the market for larger gains. The chart is very simple to use and there is nothing to buy or subscribe to.

We would make far more money when selling at the peak and buying at the bottom. There are some common parameters in the last two market peaks / bottoms.

The chart could be the best-kept secret. I guess most folks do not want to share this shocking tool to detect market crashes.

I have spent a lot of time looking for hints to detect market plunges. This could help you avoid the next big plunge that could cost you more than 30% of your investment. Market recoveries offer the best opportunity to make big money, and in this book, I describe when and how. Your money to buy this book and the time you invest in reading it could lead to huge gains. Such diligence and effort keeps on rewarding for years to come.

I have been a stock investor for over 30 years and a full-time investor for the last seven years with exhaustive stock research and performance improvements. This book is targeted to retail investors and I am one myself.

I predict that a secular bull market will be starting as early as 2017 when the two wars will finally be totally over. If the wars do not end as expected, most likely it will still happen before 2020. I have strong arguments for both scenario forecasts. You heard it here first.

The lessons from my bad experiences could be more valuable than the good ones. I achieved a huge return in 2009 in my largest taxable account and reveal my secrets here. The bottom fishing strategy could be the most profitable during the early market recovery, but we need to discover when exactly that recovery occurs.

Sectors and stocks are similar to predicting the market. Need to adjust the number of days for the moving averages to shorter duration depending on how often you rotate them. In addition, some stocks are better suited for technical analysis than others.

How this book is organized
This book has 3 sections: Technical Analysis, Market Timing and Bonus.

Most graphs and tables are in landscape orientation for both paperback and e-readers. Some graphs may not be displayed adequately on a small screen of an e-reader. E-readers may be available in the current version of Windows, so you can read ebooks on the larger screen of your PC. For better orientation, just flip the e-readers 90 degrees.

A link is usually included for these screens. Copy it to your browser to display the graphs on your PC if desirable. Instructions on how to produce some graphs are provided as you should try them out. One example is how to produce a chart on detecting market crashes.

It is easier to display some tables in landscape mode. Select a table or a graph via your e-reader to display it to fit the screen.

The font size and page size of most e-book formats can be adjusted. The unknown, special character is the "smiling face" that the current Kindle does not convert correctly as of this writing.

There are clickable links to web articles. Most of them are from my own websites and public websites such as Wikipedia. Some public links may not be available in the future as they are not under my control and my book offerings may change.

Fidelity Video provides video clips to explain some basic terms and it may require Fidelity customers to sign on in order to view them. Check the trial offer from Fidelity. YouTube offers similar video lessons.

These links extend the usefulness of this book by making available specific topics that may not be interesting to every reader. It also provides articles (most are not written by me) for more in-depth analyses.

The current version provides most of the links the paperback readers can enter into your browser. Get the same information by entering a search in Wikipedia such as Dogs of Dow.

Investopedia is another source beside Wikipedia.
http://www.investopedia.com/

'Afterthoughts' includes my additional comments and comments from others. Readers can make comments on this book's website. These comments may be included in the Afterthoughts in subsequent revisions, with the commenter's last name redacted. It is the section of the article for freer and informal discussion. It also contains some political and social issues.

There are fillers with tips and jokes (most original) to fill up the empty space of the printed book. Fillers, links and afterthoughts may disrupt the flow of reading this book. However, no readers so far ask me to take them out.

For convenience, this book uses SPY, an Exchange Traded Fund (ETF) simulating the S&P 500, as the benchmark for the market.

Annualized returns (Return * 365 / (Days between)) are used where appropriate for more meaningful comparison. To illustrate, I have a 10% return in 6 months, a 10% in a year and a 10% in 2 years. It is more meaningful to use annualized returns of 20%, 10% and 5% respectively for the 6-month return, the one-year return and the 2-year return in this example.

Usually I do not include the dividend, so you can add an estimated 1.5% to the annualized return. In addition, compound interest is not used for easier calculation, so the actual return could be even better.

About the author
I graduated from Cal. State University at San Jose in Industrial Engineering and University of Mass. in Amherst with a MS in Industrial Engineering. My last job was in IT. I have been an investor for over 30 years.

Dedication
To all retail investors and future retail investors including my grandchildren.

I sincerely hope this book will build bridges with fellow investors with different backgrounds.

Acknowledgement
Thanks to Seeking Alpha, Fidelity, Wikipedia and Investopedia for the many helpful links to enrich this book and Yahoo!Finance and Finviz.com for the tools and charts used in this book.

Important notices
© 2019-2022 Tony Pow. © Tony Pow 2015-2016 on 1st Edition.
Send Emails to pow_tony@yahoo.com.
This book is a rewrite of Applied Technical Analysis which has its first edition on 02/15.

Version	Paperback	e-Book
1.0	11/19	11/19
1.2	10/21	10/21
1.3	05/22	05/22

Book store managers can order the paper version of this book from Createspace.com.
https://tonyp4idea.blogspot.com/2020/12/book-managers.html
Book update.
https://ebmyth.blogspot.com/2020/12/updates-for-all-books.html

No part of this book can be reproduced in any form without the written approval of the author.

Disclaimer

Do not gamble with money that you cannot afford to lose. Past performance is a guideline and is not necessarily indicative of future results. All information is believed to be accurate, but there is not a guarantee. All the strategies including charts to detect market plunges described have no guarantee that they will make money and they may lose money. Do not trade without doing due diligence and be warned that most data may be obsolete. All my articles and the associated data are for informational and illustration purposes only. I'm not a professional investment counselor, a tax professional or any other field. Seek one before you make any investment decisions. Remember to consult with a registered financial adviser before making any investment decisions. The above mentioned also applies for all other advice such as on accounting, taxes, health and any topic mentioned in this book. Tax laws change all the time, so talk to your tax advisors before taking any action. Some articles may offend some one or some organization unintentionally. If I did, I'm sorry about that. I am politically and religiously neutral. I have provided my best efforts to ensure the accuracy of my articles. Data also from different sources was believed to be accurate. However, there is no guarantee that they are accurate and suitable for the current market conditions and /or your individual situations. The values of some parameters such as RSI(14) are arbitrarily set by me. I have made a lot of predictions that may not materialize. My publisher and I are not liable for any damages in using this book or its contents.

How the rate of return is calculated

They are for education purposes only, and do not make your investing decisions based on them.

Section I: Technical Analysis (TA)

Technical analysis (TA) is the analysis of the price movements and the short-term trend and possible reversal, while fundamental analysis focuses on metrics such as price/earnings ratio and debts. Traders use TA a lot and can profit by shorting stocks. Investors can use them to find the entry points and exits points and some investors only buys stocks with positive long-term trend (using SMA-200%). Many times stock analysis based on fundamentals fail when the evaluation is solely based on fundamentals. Technical Analysis (TA) has the following characteristics:

- Most of the time, TA is profitable in the short term (less than 3 months). The weather man is more accurate in tomorrow's weather rather than a month away. TA can also signal the reversals.
- It is too many signals if you have more than three TA parameters. To start, use SMA (Simple Moving Average) and RSI(14); both are available on Finviz.com without charting.
- You can combine TA with fundamentals such as a rising SMA50 with increasing Insider Purchases. For market timing, TA is a huge part, but many fundamentals should be considered too.

Technical analysis wins for the following reasons:
- Information such as a new product or a major lawsuit pending is not reflected timely in fundamentals, but rather in technical analysis. It gives us guidance in understanding the trend of a stock or even the entire market.
- Most TAs are based on accumulated data. For example, if RSI(14) is greater than 65, most likely this stock is overbought. If there is no reason for this condition, you may consider to sell it.
- When too many investors follow TA, it would become self-prophecy.
- Do not act against the trend. The fundamentalist may buy a stock when it loses 50%, the TA investor most likely will not buy it. Many times the losing stocks will lose again 25% or so. The TA investor most likely buys it on the way up.

An example. NVRO (a stock symbol) has appreciated about 100% from mid Feb. to Oct. in 2016 despite its poor fundamentals. It has a new product that could revolutionize physical healing and eliminating pain that will not be shown in the fundamentals except by the eventual Forward P/E. Technical chart can inform us of the uptrend.

Info from free websites. Use "Head and shoulder" as an example. Obtain the description by typing "Head and shoulder" in Investopedia. Obtain more info by entering same in the search under YouTube.

Overview of Technical Analysis

Technical analysis (TA) is a method of evaluating securities by analyzing statistical trends from trading activity, such as price movements and volume. It is primarily used by traders to make short- to medium-term investment decisions.

1. Key Principles of Technical Analysis
- **Price Discounts Everything** – Market prices reflect all available information, including news, earnings, and investor sentiment.
- **Prices Move in Trends** – Prices tend to follow trends rather than move randomly.
- **History Repeats Itself** – Market patterns and investor behavior tend to be repetitive.

2. Common Technical Indicators & Tools
Trend Indicators (Identify Market Direction)
- Moving Averages (SMA & EMA) –
    - SMA (Simple Moving Average): Average price over a set period (e.g., **SMA-50, SMA-200**).
    - EMA (Exponential Moving Average): Gives more weight to recent prices.
- **MACD (Moving Average Convergence Divergence)** – Shows trend strength and reversals.
- **Bollinger Bands** – Identifies volatility and overbought/oversold levels.

Momentum Indicators (Measure Speed of Price Movements)
- **RSI (Relative Strength Index)** – Measures stock momentum:
    - **Above 70** = Overbought (possible reversal down).
    - **Below 30** = Oversold (possible reversal up).
- **Stochastic Oscillator** – Similar to RSI but focuses on closing prices in relation to the high-low range.

Volume Indicators (Confirm Trends)
- **OBV (On-Balance Volume)** – Tracks volume flow to confirm trends.
- **Volume Moving Average** – Rising volume confirms strong price trends.

Support & Resistance Levels
- **Support** – A price level where demand is strong enough to prevent further decline.

- **Resistance** – A price level where selling pressure prevents further rise.

Chart Patterns (Identify Market Psychology)
- **Head and Shoulders** – Signals a trend reversal.
- **Double Top/Double Bottom** – Indicates resistance or support breakouts.
- **Triangles (Ascending/Descending/Symmetrical)** – Predicts breakouts in price direction.

3. Types of Technical Trading Strategies

Trend Following – Buying stocks in an **uptrend** and selling in a **downtrend** (e.g., using moving averages).

Breakout Trading – Buying when prices break above **resistance** or selling when they fall below **support**.

Mean Reversion – Stocks that move far from their historical average tend to return (e.g., RSI oversold levels).

Momentum Trading – Buying stocks with strong price movement (e.g., high RSI or MACD crossovers).

4. Pros & Cons of Technical Analysis

✔ **Advantages:**
- ☑ **Quick Decision Making** – Ideal for short-term traders.
- ☑ **Identifies Trends & Patterns** – Helps spot buy/sell opportunities.
- ☑ **Works in Any Market** – Can be applied to stocks, crypto, forex, and commodities.

✖ **Risks & Limitations:**
- ⚠ **Not Always Reliable** – Patterns and indicators do not guarantee future price movements.
- ⚠ **Market Manipulation** – Low-volume stocks can be influenced by large players.
- ⚠ **Over-Reliance on Charts** – Ignoring fundamentals can lead to poor long-term decisions.

5. Conclusion

Technical analysis is a valuable tool for traders but works best when combined with **risk management** and **fundamental analysis**.

1   Technical analysis (TA)

The basics

Technical analysis (a.k.a. charting) is easier to learn than you might expect. It represents the trend of the market (a stock or a group of stocks) graphically. If more investors are in the market, the market would move upwards until it changes direction. We divide the trends into short-term, intermediate-term and long-term.

The chartists usually do not consider fundamentals as they believe they have already been priced into the stock price and some fundamentals are not available to the public. To illustrate, a new drug has been discovered, the stock price of the company jumps initially by insiders purchases and the informed. Its fundamental metrics do not demonstrate this right away, but many investors are buying to boost up the stock price as evidenced by the technical indicators such as SMA for 20 or 50 days.

The volume is a confirmation. When the stock moves up or down by 10% with a low volume, the trend is not yet confirmed.

The trend of the stock price is not a straight line in most cases. Hence a trend line is usually drawn to indicate the direction of the stock. Many investors believe the stocks fluctuate in certain ranges (i.e., channels) and the chart draws the upper value (the resistance line) and the lower value (the support line). In theory, the price of a stock fluctuates within the resistance line (ceiling for understanding) and support (floor). When it reaches its support, it becomes a buy and vice versa for a sell. Most charts including Finviz.com would display these lines.

When the price passes out of the channel, it is called a breakout. Darvas, one of the oldest and most successful chartists, profited from the breakouts of the resistance line and believed the stock was close to the support line of the new channel. Hence it would be a long way up in theory.

If it were so simple, there will be no poor folks

It works most of the time, but do not place all your money on it. For chartists, 51% is great (the same for playing Black Jack). Some trends reverse very fast such as the bio drug stocks in 2015. You need to hedge your bets such as placing stop orders. Most do not want to spend their lives watching the trend from a big screen.

Most novices use too many technical indicators and lose in their performances to the professionals. Recently, most chartists were not doing all that great and I did not find many books on their success than a decade ago. It could be due to too many followers in similar setups. I verified it with my recent testing using Finviz.com.

Simple Moving Average
The basic technical indicator is SMA-N. It is the average of the last N trade sessions. To illustrate, if N is 15 and the exchange is open during this period, you need 3 weeks (21 days) of data. When N is 20 (or SMA-20), we classify it as short-term. Similarly, SMA-50 is an intermediate-term and SMA-200 is long-term. I prefer 50, 100 and 250. This trend duration is important. For example, do not want to place long-term purchases using the short-term SMA-50. There are many modifications to SMA such as giving more weight to recent data, but I have not found them any better. Finviz.com includes this information without charting (SMA-20, SMA-50 and SMA-100 in percentages).

Defining the trend periods is rather arbitrary. I use SMA-350 to detect the market plunges and SMA-100 for stocks. Weighted Moving Average weighs more weight on recent price data.

It can be used to determine whether we are in a bull, a bear or a sideways market using SMA-50 (or SMA-200 for longer term) for the market (using SPY), the sector (using an ETF for the sector and the specific stock. The trend is up when the price is above the SMA and the reversal of the trend.
https://www.youtube.com/watch?v=jdYNaE5GJ0k

The trend is your best friend
Most traders use TA for trending in a short duration. Investors can also use TA to time the entry and exit points for better potential profits. Value investors usually are patient and they do bottom fishing and they search for 'oversold' conditions using RSI(14). Again, high volume is a confirmation.

Many sites provide charting free of charge such as Yahoo!Finance. Finviz.com provides a lot of technical indicators without charting such as SMA% and RSI(14). It also provides screen searching for stocks that meet your technical analysis criteria.

Hands on
Bring up Finviz.com and enter any stock symbol such as AAPL. You can see the daily prices of AAPL from about nine months ago to today. Three SMAs (Simple Moving Average) are displayed as SMA-20, SMA-50 and SMA-200. The first two are for short-term trends. When the price is above the SMA, it is expected to be trending up. Again, the trade volume is used as a confirmation.

You can also see the resistance line and the support line drawn. In theory, the stock will trade within these lines. When it exceeds its resistance line, it is called a breakout, and vice versa for a breakdown. Sometimes it displays some technical patterns such as Cup and Shoulder and Double Down (both are positive patterns).

Select Weekly data. The Candle chart is better described than the Daily chart. Candles give us better descriptions of the price: open, close, high and low. The green color indicates the price is up for the period (a week in this example) and the red color indicates a down period.

In addition, Finviz.com includes some technical indicators in the metric section such as RSI. Most other chart sites are similar in the basics. Use Finviz's Help and select Technical Analysis for more description. Investopedia has enhanced descriptions on this topic.

TA patterns
There are many TA patterns such as Bollinger Bands and MACD. The patterns are based on the stock prices and many times they prove to be correct predictions especially on stocks with high volume and high market caps. Patterns have been repeating themselves many times as they are driven by investors.

Sites for TA
There are many free sites for charts with explanations of their technical indicators. Popular ones include BigCharts.com,

SmallCharts.com and Yahoo!Finance. Fidelity includes some unique features in its charts such as P/E.

Why I do not use TA as a primary tool for stock picking

My investing style is different from a day trader. I prefer to 'Buy Low and Sell High' instead of 'Buy High and Sell Higher'. I try to find the real bottom price. TA will not find the bottom very easily but it tracks the trend better. As a bargain hunter, I do not expect the stock will rise fast as I'm usually swimming against the tide. However, value stocks could stay in the low price for a long time (i.e., value trap). I like to select stocks that turn around as evidenced by the SMA-20 and SMA-50.

With that said, my momentum portfolio has appreciated consistently and usually has the best performing stocks among all my portfolios. It is based on the timely grade from my subscriptions plus the metrics on TA timing.

Most chartists would also tell you to buy the stocks that have broken out (i.e., higher than the resistance line) and/or stocks at their highs. Contrary to value investing, you should exit when the trend reverses. The reversal could happen very fast and hence protect your portfolio by setting up stop loss (preferably with trailing stop) orders.

My opinion. I do not want to argue whether TA is good for you or not. You need to find that out. Most likely, the day traders and very short-term traders will profit more from TA than the investors seeking value stocks for the long-term gains.

Random remarks

Even if you do not use technical analysis, you should spend some time learning it. It is better to marry fundamentals and TA. My random remarks are:
- The Institutional investors (insurance companies, pension funds, mutual funds, etc.) use TA and they MOVE the market. A lot of times it becomes a self-fulfilling prophecy. It is better to join them as most of us cannot beat them.
- Day traders take advantage of the institutional investors by spotting their trends and jumping on the wagon.

- Most TA stocks should be good sized and have large average daily volumes. I prefer to use TA on value stocks to prevent long-term losses.
- I do know some folks making big money using TA, but I know more making good money using fundamentals. Since TA predicts the market better in the shorter term, its practitioners may have to pay higher taxes (in today's tax laws) in taxable accounts.
- Our objective should be making money with the least risk. Once you claim to belong to a certain group of either Fundamental or TA, you will be biased and forget your primary objective in investing.
- TA tracks the last two big market plunges (2000 and 2007) pretty well. The chart will not warn you right away for the upcoming plunge (as it depends on past data) to avoid the initial losses, but they will warn you to avoid bigger losses.
- You can use TA to short the stock, the sector, the country or the market.
- Risk management (with stops to reduce losses and trailing stops for rising stocks) and trade positions (more positions on stocks with better potential) could make you a fortune, even if you have only 50% correct.
- Your desire, passion, discipline, knowledge and hand-on skill (including learning from your successes and failures) are the keys to success. A well-tested strategy and TA tools to time the trend of a stock, sector and the market are the tools.

Afterthoughts
Besides searching for stocks that have potential breakouts, we should check the stocks we own for potential breakdowns.
Technical Analysis tutorial.
https://www.YouTube.com/watch?v=GENBVwV8PMs

SMA tutorial.
https://www.YouTube.com/watch?v=Na-ctpPsnks

Links
Fidelity video: Technical Analysis
https://www.fidelity.com/learning-center/technical-analysis/chart-types-video

2   Examples of using TA

I have outlined how we can spot market plunges using TA and I use it to monitor the market every three months or so (I recommend doing it every month and even more frequently when the market is risky). Here is an example of how to use it to trade individual stocks.

I have to admit I do not use TA that much on individual stocks and clearly I am not an expert in TA. If this article stirs up your interest, read more books or attend seminars / classes on TA. However, this book describes the basic and most useful technical indicators. There are many good and free articles from Investopedia on this topic. Personally, I prefer to seek fundamentally sound companies at bargain prices and wait for their full appreciation. It has been proven to me many times over.

TA is very useful for momentum and day traders. With the rising volume, you can detect that the stocks are traded by managers of mutual funds, hedge funds, insurance companies and pension funds, and you profit by riding on their wagons.

Some stocks are good for TA. Usually, they are larger companies with above-average volumes and are fundamentally sound. Avoid the stocks that are trending downwards unless you're bottom fishing. Let me pick CSCO (a cyclical stock) for an illustration. I bought it several times in 2012. I sold some in 2013 and 2014 making good profits. This is quite different from what short-term traders would use during the following:

The green line is a 50-day simple moving average (SMA) for the following chart using one year data. Buy the stock when it is above its SMA and sell when it is below. Following the chart would make good money based on this simple rule. Also, practice the strategy "Sell on May 1, Buy back on Nov. 1".

Not all stocks follow this profitable pattern. Fundamentalists may try to pick the bottom in late July while chartists enter positions on its upward trend. The chartists have an advantage to stay away from stocks in their downward trend.

Exponential Moving Average has better predictable power as it weighs more on recent prices. Some indicators / patterns work better in specific market conditions – all markets are different.

Volume is important as a confirmation. If the price of a stock is up with thin volume, the rise is questionable and it could be manipulated.

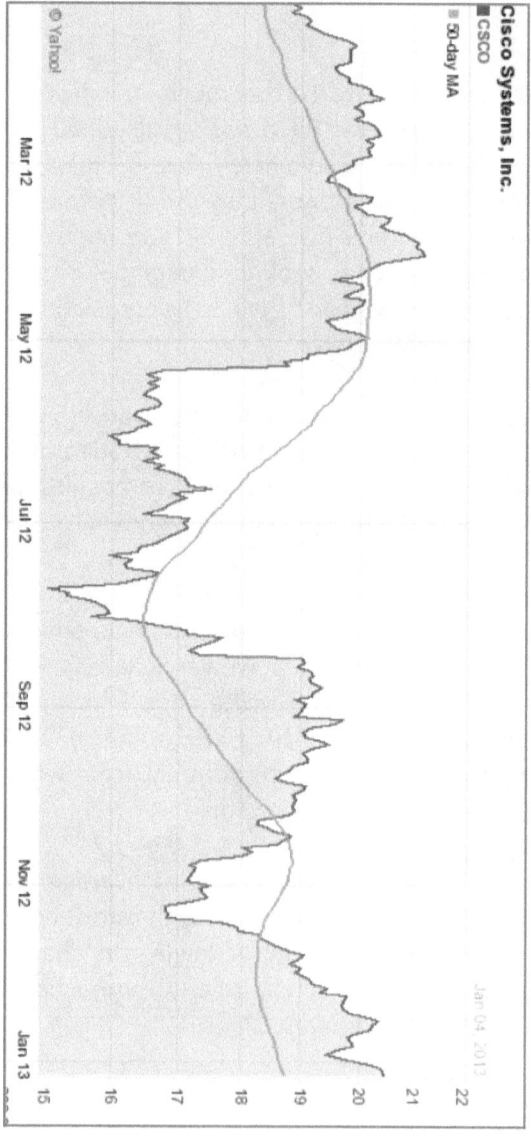

Table: CSCO 50-day SMA   Source: Yahoo!Finance (https://ebmyth.blogspot.com/2020/09/table-csco-50-day-sma.html)

We can improve the trades by:
- Use a different moving average in the number of days (50 in this example) and other indicators such as EMA (a moving average that weighs higher on more recent data). It may improve prediction accuracy and/or cut down on the number of trades. RSI(14) suggests overbought / oversold conditions.

- Instead of selling the stock for cash, consider selling the stock short. Selling short is definitely not for beginners.

- The accuracy is usually improved by a separate chart for the sector the stock belongs to and another one for the market. For CSCO, you can use an ETF for network companies and SPY (or a similar ETF) to represent the market.

   In theory and in theory only, when both the stock, the sector that the stock is in and the market all move down, the stock price has a high chance that it would move down, and vice versa.

   We use the 50 days (in SMA) for short-term holding of stocks (20 for even shorter holding periods and 200 days for longer holding periods). Personally, I use 30 days for the sector ETF. Again, 'Days' is actually 'Trade Sessions'.

TA is not for most fundamentalists but it should be used

For a bargain hunter like me, TA would not benefit me a lot for picking stocks at their bottoms. I would try to pick up CSCO with prices ranging from 15-17 and all well below the moving average line, but TA would not show me a Buy signal. However, for short-term swing traders TA is a Godsend.

To me, TA is a good indicator for growth, momentum and for short-term trading. Some fundamentalists may use TA for entry and exit points. Some recommend buying the stock when the price is above the SMA-200 (same as when SMA-200% is positive and that can be readily obtained from Finviz.com).

It should be profitable for using the 'Buy High and Sell Higher' strategy, provided you protect your profits effectively. This is also called 'Buy at a reasonable cost'. One's opinion.

In selecting a tool, you have to understand how, and why to use it and whether it fits your investing style. I use TA for market timing for the entire market more than on individual stocks. When I have more time, I probably would use TA more frequently.

Most of us cannot spot the bottom of a stock; I have had some success but most likely they were due to luck. When a stock is moving up from the bottom, there is a good chance it will move further up. TA shows it and the volume confirms it.

Conclusion
Even a fundamentalist like me can benefit a lot by using TA. This book touches on the very basics of TA.

Besides monitoring the fundamentals of the stocks you bought once every 6 months, you should analyze their technical indicators more often (1 month to 3 months depending on your available time). When the market is risky (close to the SMA average), run the SMA chart more frequently (say once a week).

Rule-based trading:
https://www.youtube.com/watch?v=GAH9EyydEsM

---

3   Easy TA without charts

Bring up Finviz.com from your browser. Enter the stock you're evaluating. SMA-200% stands for Simple Moving Average of the last 200 trade sessions. RSI(14)% is the relative strength index for the last 14 trade sessions.

The following is just a suggestion with conservative parameters. Adjust the parameters according to your risk tolerance and requirements. Do not buy the stock with SMA-200% is < 0 (trending down), SMA-200% > 40 (peaking), or RSI(14)% > 65 (overbought).
Link: RSI: https://www.youtube.com/watch?v=VH84ppzmq9Q

4 More on technical analysis

This chapter describes some TA indicators that can help us. Click on the following links for a better description.

- Finviz.com.
  It has SMA20%, SMA50% and SMA200% to represent the short-term, intermediate-term and the long-term indicator. SMA stands for Simple Moving Average and n for days for the duration of the average (for example, 20 days for SMA20%).

  If you are a long-term investor, use SMA-200% (or SMA-350%). Using SMA-20% would cause a lot of sells / reentries, which costs more in trading fees.

  Buy when the price is above the Moving Average line and sell when the price is below it. Finviz.com provides the percent of moving above the moving average to indicate just how much the price deviates from the average.

  If you hold the stock for an average of 50 days, use SMA50%, and so on. If you hold stocks for an average of 90 days, you have to create your own SMA using one of the many websites including Yahoo!Finance and specify 90 days for the period.

  Try other similar technical indicators such as EMA, which is supposed to weigh more on the more recent data. A weather man can predict tomorrow's weather better than the weather a week away.

- RSI(14) indicates whether the stock is overbought or oversold. RSI oscillates between zero and 100. Traditionally, and according to Wilder (the author of this method), RSI is considered overbought with a value above 70 and oversold with a value below 30 as described in the article.

  When it is oversold, most likely the stock will fall, and vice versa.

(http://stockcharts.com/school/doku.php?id=chart_school:technical_indicators:relative_strength_index_rsi)

Click here for another article.
(http://financial-dictionary.thefreedictionary.com/Relative+Strength+Index)

- Cup and handle is a popular indicator of when the stock price would surge.
  (http://www.investopedia.com/terms/c/cupandhandle.asp)

- Double bottom indicates that the stock will move up.
  (http://stockcharts.com/school/doku.php?id=chart_school:chart_analysis:chart_patterns:double_bottom_revers)

  It shows a double bottom for Apple in 2013.

- A trading strategy:
  https://www.youtube.com/watch?v=asDBegQaupM

#Fillers
"Hold" rating from analysts means "Sell as fast as you can". Very seldom, there is a "Sell".

Filler: The 0.5%
The world has been controlled by 0.5% who are the wealthiest and make the rules of the world. These folks own US businesses and EU businesses, and they make money in every way and everywhere they see opportunities. The following link and Tesla's mega factory in China forced me to think; it is a case of Biden vs the 0.5%.
https://finance.yahoo.com/news/citigroup-hire-1-700-people-093000440.html

5   Using Finviz.com as a screener example

The following is an example. Fine tune the selection criteria according to your personal criteria and risk tolerance.

- Bring up Finviz.com from your browser. Select Screener, the third tab. As of 3/24/2015, we have 7066 stocks.

- For illustration, we would like to find stocks with double bottoms, a positive technical indicator. If not using the All tab, select the Technical tab. Select Pattern and then Double Bottom. Now we have 257 stocks.

- Select the Fundamental tab (next to the Technical tab). Select Forward P/E and then select "under 20". Now, we have 86 stocks.

- Select Debt/Equity less than .5. Now, we have 45 stocks. Some industries are traditionally high in debts, so you can use 'less than 1'.

- Select EPS growth Q-to-Q over 10%. Now, we have 19 stocks.

- Select the Description tab. Select Country to USA. Now, we have 17 stocks.

- Select Price > 1. Select Avg. Volume "Over 100K". Select Float Short "Under 10%. Select Analyst Recom. "Buy or better". Now we have 9 stocks.
  Now we can evaluate them one by one using Fundamental Analysis, Intangible Analysis, Qualitative Analysis and Technical Analysis. The purpose of screening is to filter the 7000 stocks to a small number (9 stocks in this case).

Skip the stocks that have the Earnings Date within 2 weeks. If you already have too many stocks in the same industry, skip that stock. Click the stock to get more metrics of the stock. You can save the screen when you register with Finviz.com. It is free. Check the performance in 3 months or so.

Try other technical indicator such as "Head and Shoulder".

6   Finviz's parameters

Most metrics are described in Finviz (via Help), Investopedia and/or Wikipedia and my chapters on P/E and fundamental metrics if available. We use the metrics for screening stocks and then evaluating the screened stocks.

The following are my personal comments and why I feel some metrics are more important than the others. Personally, I divide the metrics into fundamentals and technical, which are more important for long-term investors and short-term investors respectively.

Compare the ratios to the companies in the same sector (industry) and also its averages from the last few years (5 preferable) from many other websites such as Fidelity.

From your browser, enter Finviz.com. Enter a symbol (I used ABEO for discussion). A chart is displayed with the prices and volumes for the last eleven months. SMAs (Single Moving Average) are displayed sometimes with other technical indicators. Intraday, Daily and Weekly options are available for day traders, short-term traders and long-term traders respectively. I prefer Candle – Advanced for drawing charts.

Besides the chart and the metrics described next, it describes what the company does, analysts' recommendations (I prefer Fidelity's Equity Summary Score), insiders' trading and articles that are good for intangible and qualitative analysis. Many free websites such as Yahoo!Finance provide a list of articles about the company.

"Financial Highlights and Statements" are materials for more in-depth analysis and they were more important decades ago when most financial ratios had not been calculated for you. It is important for investors with good knowledge in financial accounting. The current version also includes the basic balance sheet, income statement and cash flow for the current (TTM) and the last two years. Click on the following YouTube links for more detail.

Balance: https://www.youtube.com/watch?v=DMv9JC_K37Y

Income: https://www.youtube.com/watch?v=0--AvwZablQ
Cash flow: https://www.youtube.com/watch?v=hMBN6yTIDb0

A section on Insider Trading is also included. Do not be alarmed when insiders dump small quantities of the stocks. Buying large quantities (e.g., insider transaction more than 5%) at prices close to the market price could be favorable news.

The following metrics are roughly based on the flow of Finviz from top to bottom and left to right. I skip those metrics that I believe are not too important. You can also place your cursor on the metric to retrieve the description from Finviz or via Finviz's Help. Some metrics are left blank to indicate they are not applicable (for example, zero, negative or not available). For example, the Debt/Equity of YRCW in 1/2019 is blank (same as null) due to its negative Equity. From Yahoo!Finance at the time of writing, it has a total debt of 888M.

- **Index**. Most of us trade stocks in the three major exchanges in the USA. Stocks listed over-the-counter are too risky for most of us. Skip the stocks in local exchanges and foreign exchanges unless you are an expert on these stocks and/or have insightful (not illegal info from insiders) information. I screen the stocks and then ignore the stocks that are not in the Dow, NASDAQ and Amex. Other screeners may let you select a group of exchanges.
- **Market Cap** (MC). To me, stocks below 50M are risky even though they could be very profitable. Ensure the Avg. Volume is at least 10,000 shares and / or your order is less than 1% of the average volume. Some small stocks are controlled by the owners and have small volumes. You cannot trade these stocks easily.

Float = Outstanding shares – Insider shares

Usually, Float does not matter as they are typically the same. However, it does for small companies with large insider shares. Most of these owners do not want to sell their family businesses and hence they reduce the chance of being acquired entirely or partially for good prices. In this case, you

may have to hold this kind of stock for a long time or you may have to sell it at a very unfavorable price.
- If **Forward P/E** (a.k.a. Expected P/E) is not provided, use the P/E which is based on the trailing last 12 months (TTM). Alternatively, calculate the E by using the E from P/E and multiplying it by its growth rate. It may not be seasonally adjusted. I prefer using Forward P/E as it provides a better predictability power to me. Successful investing is usually a result of correct guessing the future earnings.

Finviz.com leaves the P/E blank (same as null) if the earnings are negative. In this case, I would check out Yahoo!Finance's EV / EBITDA, which also considers taxes, cash and interests. The blank condition also happens in some other metrics such as negative assets (very seldom).

Earnings Yield is equal to E/P. I call it 'True Earnings Yield' for EBITDA / EV. It is easier to understand. Compare Earnings Yield or True Yield to the annual dividend yield of a 10-year Treasury – with the low interest rate in 2021, skip this comparison for this year.

E/P is easier in screening and sorting the screened stocks. If you use P/E instead of E/P, you need to screen or sort stocks with a clause "P/E > 0".

When the P/E is less than 5, be careful and there may be a reason why it is so low. Many bankrupting companies have low P/Es at one time before their stock prices go to zero..

Compare the P/E or Forward P/E with the average P/E for the sector and its average P/E for the last 5 years that are available from Fidelity.com. Some sectors such as technology have high P/Es (25 for me). If the sector is cyclical, the earnings could be affected.

When the prospect of the company is good such as Tesla in 2020, ignore P/E. Investors are betting on the future. Do not short these rocket stocks.
- **Cash / share**. It is used to calculate Pow P/E and Pow EY when EV/EBITDA for the stock is not available. To illustrate, if the

stock is $10 and it has $10 cash / share without debt (i.e., Debt/Equity = 0), most likely it is underpriced as you can get the whole company for nothing. You should find out why the price is so low. It could be the market ignoring the stock, or there is a serious event happening such as a major lawsuit. P/C is a better choice than Cash/Share; the lower the better.

- **Dividend %** is useful for income investors. The payout ratio should not be more than 30% except for matured companies. Most developing companies and tech companies plough back the profits into research and development, and hence they do not pay dividends.
- **Recs**. Select stocks with 1 or 2. Do not base your stock selection on this recommendation alone. There have been many bad recommendations that could cost you a fortune in losses. Use Fidelity's Equity Summary Score instead.
- **PEG** is a measure of the growth of P/E and hence a growth metric (the other ones are Sales Growth Q-Q and Earnings Growth Q-Q). It is similar to P/E, but it takes the expected earnings growth rate into account. The lower value is better as long as earnings is positive. If earnings is negative, then the reverse is true. It is a defect in using P/E and PEG and that's why I recommend EY (Earnings Yield) and EYG, Earnings Yield Growth.

  If there are two companies with the same P/E, the one with a better PEG ratio is better. For similar logic, if two companies have the same E/P, the company with higher Earnings Growth (EPS Q/Q) would be better.
- **P/B**. Book value (= Total Assets − Total Liabilities) may not include intangible assets such as patents. Do not trust it 100%, so is ROE and other metrics which are based on the book value. Negative equity is possible when Total Liabilities is more than Total Assets. This popular metric is outdated for most matured companies as it is now made up of more intangible assets including patents, management, the quality of their employees, brand names, market share, partners, free cash flow and customer base to name a few.
- **P/S**. If two companies are unprofitable, this ratio could be more useful. A retail company such as Walmart is very different from a research company in P/S. This metric is only meaningful for stocks within the same sector or related sectors.

- **P/FCF**. I prefer it to be greater than 0 and less than 50 for value investors. Most metrics can be manipulated easily, but not this one. This is a major metric to avoid bankrupting companies.
- **Sales Q/Q** reduces the seasonal deviation. To illustrate, retail sales for the Christmas season should be compared to the same season in the prior year.
- **EPS Q/Q**. Same as above. I prefer the growth of EPS over Sales. Both of these Q/Q ratios are growth metrics. When a company terminates its unprofitable product(s), its Sales Q/Q could be down but its EPS Q/Q could be up. In 2000, many internet companies had great Sales Q/Qs but negative EPS Q/Qs.

  Q/Q comparison (quarter to quarter) takes out the seasonal variations as Sales Q/Q. I prefer both Sales Q/Q and EPS Q/Q increase. When EPS Q/Q increases far higher than Sales Q/Q, it could mean the EPS Q/Q could be temporary such as the oil company when the oil price rockets.

  When the company buys its own shares, EPS could be misleading as E is fixed and the number of shares is reduced. In most cases, the fundamentals of the company have not changed.

  In 2021, many companies such as many energy stocks have incredible EPS Q-Q and most of their Forward P/E are better than the P/E. They could be momentum play unless they are sustainable.
- Positive **Insider** Transactions are favorable. Sometimes, they are misleading. Need to scroll to the end of the screen and check out more info there. If the transactions are outdated such as 3 months or so ago, and or they are purchases in a similar amount than the sales a while ago, they are not important. Insiders know the company better than us.

  So is **Institutional Transactions** as institutional investors move the market. Most institutional investors do not trade small stocks, and hence this metric is not important for small cap stocks.
- Insider Own, Shares Outstanding and Shares **Float** determine the number of shares that are available for trading. The stock with a small Float and a high Insider Own limits trading and the

stock, and hence it should be avoided in most cases. Also, compare your trade positions for this kind of stock to their Avg. Volumes.
- **Profit Margin**. I prefer it over Gross Margin and Oper. Margin which does not include interest expenses and taxes. When you sell software, the Gross Margin is high as it does not include development, support and marketing, etc. A retail store has low Gross Margin. It all depends on the industry, and hence it is better to compare companies in the same industry.
- **Short Float**. I prefer it to be less than 10%. If it is greater than 10%, the shorters could find something wrong with the company. If it is over 25%, I would check the fundamentals and any important events such as a major lawsuit. If they are good, I would buy it expecting a short squeeze potential. It is risky but it has been proven profitable in some of my trades.
- Technical metrics: SMA-20, SMA-50 and SMA-200. Finviz expresses them in convenient percentages. If they are all positive, it means the trend is up. SMA-20 and SMA-50 are a short-term trend indicator and SMA-200 is a long-term trend indicator. If you are a short-term swing investor, stick with the short-term trend and vice versa. The first two are also used as momentum grades. Many long-term investors do not buy stocks when the SMA-200% is negative. Some buy stocks when both SMA-20 and SMA-50 are positive and SMA-20 crosses SMA-50,. Some sell the owned stocks when both SMA-20 and SMA-50 are negative and SMA-20 crosses SMA-50. Some use SMA-50 and SMA-200 instead. They are called the Golden Cross and the Death Cross.
- **RSI(14)**. If it is greater than 65%, it is overbought to me. If it is under 30%, it is under-bought for me to me. Some use 5% up or down than my percentages. Use it as a reference. Most stocks making new heights are always overbought, and many of these stocks keep on rising. I recommend using trailing stops to protect your profits on rising stocks.
- **Beta**. A volatile stock fluctuates a lot. Higher beta stocks are good for short-term traders. A beta of 1 means the stock would fluctuate with the market, and it is more volatile if it is higher than 1. For volatile stocks (higher than 1), the stops should be higher. For example, if your stops are normally 10%, you may want to use 15% or even higher for volatile stocks.

- **Perf**. If the stock lost more than 50%, there is a good chance it could be a candidate for bottom fishing, or it could be heading to bankruptcy. Need more research if you want to buy these risky stocks.
- Management performance is measured by **ROE**. It is also judged by **Analysts' Rec.** and Institutional Ownership (except for small companies). The confidence of their own ability, the company and its sector are measured by Insider Ownership and Insider Purchases.

    ROE = Net Income / Average Shareholder's Equity

    According to Investopedia, a normal ROE for utilities should be 10% while high tech companies should be 15%. Compare this ratio and many other ratios with its peers that are available from many sites including Fidelity.
- Avoid all companies that are going to bankrupt at all costs. Debt/Equity, P/FCF, Cash/Sh., P/B, Profit Margin, Forward P/E, Short Float, RSI(14), SMA20% and SMA50 would give us some hints. Need to summarize all the info and study many other factors such as obsoleting products (including drugs going to be generic). Study articles which are available from Finviz and many other sites.
- Unless you have concrete information, do not buy stocks a week or so before the Earnings Date (available in Finviz). It is seldom to make great profits when the announcement is better than the expected as the stock price is usually priced in, and the reverse could hurt the stock price a lot.

More useful information:
- The price chart. It has a lot of features such as the resistance line. Some charts include technical indicators such as double top (a bearish warning) and double bottom (a bullish sign).
- Description under the symbol. It briefly describes what the company (sector and industry) does and its country of registration. You want to buy a stock within a sector that is trending up. For example, according to Finviz Apple is in the Consumer Goods sector and the Electronic Equipment industry.

If you do not want to buy foreign stocks, skip it if it is not listed in the US exchange or headquartered in a foreign country. Buying a foreign stock could be profitable, but risky due to the currency fluctuation, lack of regulations, and politics (such as Russia in 2022 and China in 2021). Some foreign stocks ask you to pay additional taxes when you sell them. Some foreign companies listed in the U.S. exchanges take out a good portion of the dividends.

- Articles on the company for qualitative analysis.
- Insider trading. Pay more attention to the insider purchases at market prices. Use common sense.
- The last line lets you open Yahoo!Finance and other sites.

Other important sites

Yahoo!Finance.
From Statistics, you can find Enterprise Value / EBITDA. I call it True Yield when I flip them to EBITDA / Enterprise Value. In case it is not available, I use Earnings Yield. In my spreadsheet without considering the cell designations,

=IF (Earnings Yield = "", True Yield, Earnings Yield)

Fidelity
Compare the P/E of the average PE of the last 5 years by using spreadsheets.
Cheaper By Historically =IF(PE="","",(Avg. of 5-year PE -PE)/Avg. of 5-year PE)

Compare the P/E of companies in the same sector. In my spreadsheet for demonstration,
Cheaper By To the peers =IF(PE="","",(Industry PE - PE)/Industry PE)

Your broker's website

Your broker website should have plenty of tools to analyze stocks. As of Dec., 2018, Fidelity lets you use their extensive research free by opening an account with no position restriction. I describe some of their metrics that should be beneficial to your research.

- Equity Summary Score. Potentially good buy when it is 7 (8 for conservative investors) or higher. With some exceptions, you should avoid buy or short stocks if the score is 3 or below. The stocks ranking from 4 to 6 could be turnaround candidates if they are supported by good Q/Q Earnings and/or good news. The above are my suggestions.

- The 5-year averages are good yardsticks. For example, in Dec., 2018, C's P/E is about 9 and the average for the last 5 years is 14. Hence it is a value buy.

Other sources

If you have other sources (most require a subscription or being a customer), skip the stocks that have one of the failing grades. The exceptions are a new positive development and increased insider purchases.

Vendor	Grade	Fail
Fidelity	Equity Summary Score	< 7
IBD	Composite grade	< 50
Value Line	Proj. 3-5 yr. return. Also, its composite rating	< 3%
Zacks	Rank	5
VectorVest	VST	< 0.7

You may be able to find Value Line and IBD in your local library. Try out the free stock reports from your broker first. Finviz and Seeking Alpha should have articles (now fewer free articles from Seeking Alpha) on stocks and earnings conferences, which could have important information after separating from the "welcome" and garbage talks.

Yahoo!Finance has good info. "EV/EBITDA" is better than "P/E" as it considers debts and cash. Most use Earnings from the last 12 months, which has poorer predictability than Forward Earnings to me.

When negative values such as Equity in Finviz.com, we need to adjust many related metrics or do not use them at all.

MarketWatch.com has many articles on the market in general and personal investing.

If the stock is close to the Earnings Date (found in Finviz.com), you should avoid trading the stock; as earnings could have a big swing for the stock price. Consult Zacks' ranking which is currently free for individual stocks.

Gurus

It is nice to know how gurus would rate the interested stocks. GuruFocus is a good source but requires subscription. NASDAQ is a simplified version. Bring up Nasdaq.com from your browser. Select "Investing" and then "Guru Screeners". On the third selection, enter the stock symbol such as THO. Click "Go". You will find how 10 or so gurus would evaluate this stock in theory. Click "Detailed Analysis" for each guru.

Quick and dirty

Many times we need to evaluate a stock fast such as taking action due to some development. Or, when you have over 30 stocks from your screen, you may want to reduce the number by using the following two methods.

Refer to my other article "Simplest way to evaluate stocks". The following should take a few minutes. Bring up Finviz.com and enter the stock symbol.

Using SWKS on 6/10/16 to illustrate, Forward P/E is about 11 (fine between 3 and 25), Debt/Eq. is 0 (fine less than .5), ROE is 30% (fine greater than 5%) and P/PCF is 31 (fine if not negative).

Also, check out Market Cap, Avg. Volume, Dividend, Short Float (fine between 0% and 10%), Country and Industry. Judging from the above, it is a buy.

If you have more time, check out the following: Recom. (Ok if less than 2.5), P/B (fine between .5 and 4), Sales Q/Q (fine if not negative), EPS Q/Q (fine if not negative), Cash/Sh (compare it to Debt/Sh) and Profit Margin (fine >5%). Check some articles described for this stock.

5-minute stock evaluation

It takes even less time than the above "Quick and Dirty". However, I recommend you should spend more time researching stocks.

- From Finviz.com, enter the stock or ETF symbol. Look at the number of reds in metrics. If there are more than greens, most likely it is not a good stock.
- It should be fine if Fidelity's Equity Summary Score is greater than 8.

If you have more time, I recommend you to check the following:

- Check out Forward P/E (E>0 and P/E < 20), Debut / Equity (< 50%) and P/FCF (not in red color).
  If time is allowed, replace Forward P/E with True P/E (same as "EV/EBITDA"), which is available from Yahoo!Finance and other sources.
- SMA20 (or SMA50 for longer holding period). If SMA20 is > 10%, it is trending up.
- It is fine if the Insider Transaction is positive.
- Be cautious on foreign stocks and low-volume stocks.
- If most of the above are positive, it is likely a buy. As in life, nothing is 100% certain.

Links

PEG: http://en.wikipedia.org/wiki/PEG_ratio
Short %:
http://www.investopedia.com/university/shortselling/shortselling1.asp#axzz2LNDvpemo

Openinsider:	http://www.openinsider.com/
Finviz:	http://Finviz.com/
terms:	http://www.Finviz.com/help/screener.ashx
Insider Cow:	http://www.insidercow.com/
Current Ratio:	http://en.wikipedia.org/wiki/Current_ratio
Cash Flow:	https://www.youtube.com/watch?v=1v8hRZ36--c
Balance sheet:	https://www.youtube.com/watch?v=DZjU0CHKyV4

How to find quality stocks.
http://seekingalpha.com/article/2381395-how-to-identify-quality-stocks-and-is-there-really-alpha-to-be-had

7 Using Fidelity

Click "Research and News" and then "Stock". Simple charting and advanced charting are both provided.

Hints:

- Fidelity provides suggested stops.
- Click on the Support and Resistance under Technical Analysis to display the Resistance Line (upper limit). Click on the Resistance Line and you can get the Support Line (lower limit).
- Click on Advanced Chart and then click on "learn how to use the chart".
- Under Advanced Chart, select Draw and Trend Line. Select the upper line by touching the highest points and do the same for the lower line.

#Filler: Future jobs
American blue-collar workers are facing a hard time for sure from driverless cars/trucks to robots. The future is also bleak for many professionals such as financial advisors, accountants, pharmacists...due to AI and cheap computing. The future will be owned by stock owners and the middle class will have jobs to make devices / software to remove jobs of the above workers. It may happen in our children or grandchildren's generation, and we can see it from above or below depending on what we did in life. LOL.

8   Bollinger Bands

Bollinger Bands have been proven useful for traders. In theory, the stock is traded between the upper band and the lower band forming an envelope. For more info, click the following link.

http://www.investopedia.com/terms/b/bollingerbands.asp
https://www.youtube.com/watch?v=wfPf-KBuQH0

The following chart was drawn by Yahoo!Finance for CSCO from 8/7/2012 to 8/7/2014 selecting Bollinger Bands for the 50 days as a parameter. If you trade more often, use 20 days. If the chart is too small to display on your screen, enter the following in your PC's browser.
http://ebmyth.blogspot.com/2014/08/screen-csco-bollinger-bands-50.html

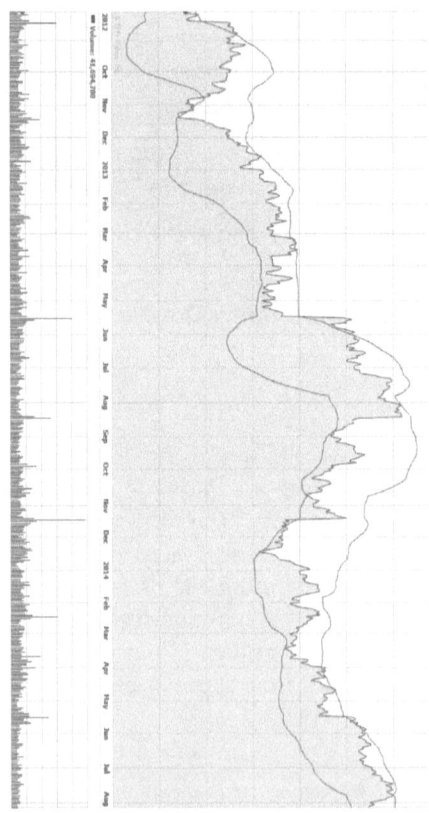

Bollinger Bands 50 Days.   Source: Yahoo!Finance

You buy the stock when the price is close to the lower band and sell the stock when it is close to the upper band.

When the stock price passes the upper band, it is called a breakout. Similar for the stock falling below the lower band. From the above, we should make some good money.

It is advisable to use at least one more technical indicator. I recommend the RSI(14), which is also accessible from Yahoo!Finance or similar sites. When it is above 70, it is overbought, so I recommend selling the stock. When it is below 30, it is oversold, so I recommend buying the stock. However, fundamentals have not been considered. Some stocks just go to zero and some just surge.

9   MACD

MACD, Moving Average Convergence Divergence, is an effective momentum (i.e., short-term) indicator used by most traders. When the stock price is crossing above the zero line, it is a buy and vice versa. It may give false signals in sideways fluctuation.
###
Again, try to master SMA and RSI(14) first. Using too many indicators usually harms you more than helps you. You can use Finviz.com to search stocks with technical indicators.

10   Double Tops

The following is the chart to use double tops to detect the last market peak in 2007.

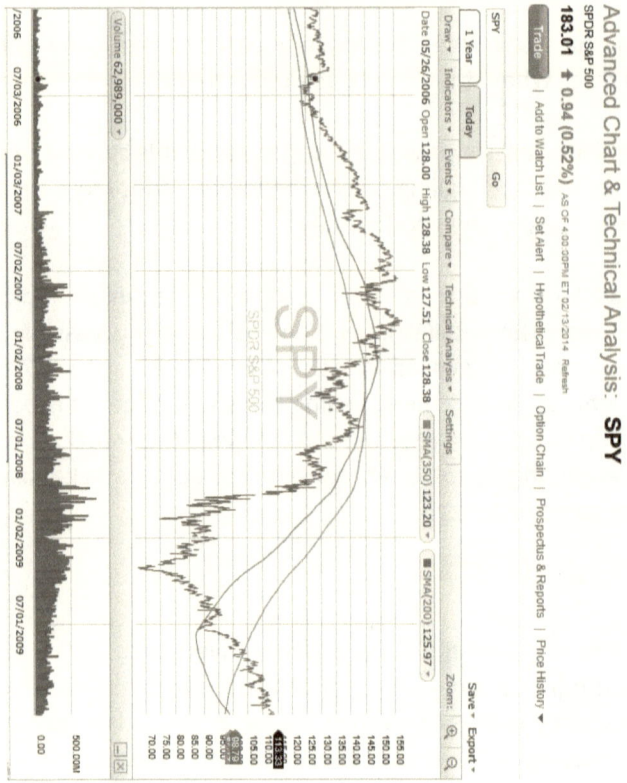

SPY: SMA.   Source: Fidelity

If you have a small screen on your e-reader, produce a similar graph using Yahoo!Finance. Enter SPY and select Technical Indicator. Select SMA and 350 days. Select the date from 1/3/2006 to 1/3/2010. Do another graph with SMA-200.

Critical dates

Table: Vital Dates

Market Plunge	Peak	Bottom	Indicator Exit	Indicator Reenter
2007	10/12/07	03/06/09	01/03/08	09/08/09

The following were obtained from my naked eyes to obtain the data from the graph. They are not accurate but are fine for discussion.

Top	Date	SPY
First	07/17/07	155
Second	10/11/07	157
Difference	86	1%
Selected	10/11/07	
Peak	10/12/07	

The SMA-350 indicator suggested us to exit the market on 01/03/08, about 83 days past the peak (10/12/07). Double Top is a better indicator here as it told us only one day before the peak. Will it happen again? Only time can tell.

Double Bottom

Again, the following is from my naked eyes to obtain the data from the graph.

Bottom	Date	SPY
First	03/17/08	127
Second	07/15/08	122
Difference	120	-4%
Selected	07/15/08	
Bottom	03/06/09	

Arbitrarily, I use the absolute difference of 5% or less to determine the double bottom condition (the absolute % of the second bottom to the first bottom).

The SMA-350 indicator suggests us to reenter the market on 09/08/09, about 186 days past the bottom (03/06/09). Double Bottom tells us to reenter the market about 234 days after the bottom. Hence, double bottom as defined here is not a good indicator.

It is interesting that the difference of days is 120. If we use 100 days as the threshold, then it is not qualified to be a double bottom.

We may want to use the earlier of either the chart or the double bottom to determine when to reenter.

Is SMA-350 better than SMA-200?

From the graph in this article, I conclude that SMA-200 has more noises that tell you to exit and reenter (or the other way) more often than SMA-350. It is logical as SMA-350 uses 350 days (vs 200) for the moving average.

However, SMA-200 tells you to reenter the market earlier from the actual bottom. Hence, it is more profitable at least for the market plunge in 2007. For the next plunge, I would use SMA-350 to exit the market and SMA-200 to reenter the market. Is it just coincident?

Link
Double Tops:
http://www.investopedia.com/terms/d/doubletop.asp

Double Tops Video.
https://www.youtube.com/watch?v=b-PaSDJiG2U

11   Other TA indicators/patterns

They are briefly mentioned here. Click on the links or use Investopedia for more descriptions.

Double Bottom is a bullish pattern as the support line is stronger than the resistance line.
Double Top is the opposite and is a bearish pattern. I prefer the price of the second top is less than the price of the first top. It seems there is no enough investment in this stock to break out of the second top.

Resistance and Support. The stock is supposed to fluctuate between an imaginary zone of resistance and support. Short-term traders may sell when the price is close to the resistance line and close any short positions when it is close to the support line. However, breakouts from this zone are possible and many traders trade stocks on breakouts. It is a little similar to 52-week highs and lows. The trend line indicates the trend of the stock.

Cup and handle is a bullish pattern. The stock price peaks and then forms a shape of a cup and handle.

Head & Shoulder is a bearish pattern while the reversed Head & Shoulder is a bullish pattern. It signals that the peak (the head) has been reached and the second top (the shoulder) has failed to reach the previous peak.

Stochastic Oscillator. It is similar to RSI(14). Many traders use this indicator. If it is above 65, it is overbought. If it is below 30, it is oversold. In general, I would trade on an uptrend when the stock is moving from 60 to 85; it depends on how volatile the stock is. It is better to use with other indicators and as a reference.

To illustrate when to buy, one suggestion is to buy when this indicator changes to an uptrend while the price is still going down.

Many traders follow these technical indicators and SMA. They could become "self-fulfilled" prophecies.

Link

Chart patterns. https://www.youtube.com/watch?v=o6hZma0bajE
More: https://www.youtube.com/watch?v=aRlWle9smww
Resistance: https://www.youtube.com/watch?v=C2qRW9_via4

12   Peaking and Overbought

This chapter is an extension of the last one. The following indicators are not very reliable and they should be used as secondary indicators. However, exiting from the peak could make you more money if the signal is correct. When the price is 9% over the simple moving average SMA-350, the market may be peaking. This ratio is defined by:

(Price – Moving Average) / Moving Average.

When the RSI(14) is over 65%, the market could be overbought (i.e. highly valued). This ratio can be found on Finviz.com with SPY or another ETF that represents the market as the stock symbol. It is defined as:

RSI = 100 - 100/(1 + RS)

where RS = Average of x days' up closes / Average of x sessions
RSI(14) is the relative strength index using last 14 trade sessions.

The reentry point is less than -31% for the SMA-350 ratio and less than 25% for the RSI(14). Again, they are used for a guideline only.

Suggested Actions

Peaking and overbought conditions indicate the market is overvalued. My suggestion is not to sell all positions except those stocks that are overvalued or have met your objectives. Place stop orders to protect profits. I recommend 5% below the current price and 10% for volatile stocks (10% and 15% are fine in today's volatile market). When the stock price rises, change the stop orders accordingly. When the stock is sold, accumulate cash until these conditions change.

I recommend to use the cash to buy CDs and short-term, bonds that are investment grade. Save some cash to buy contra ETFs when the market is plunging. 2008 was not a good year for bonds, but 2009 was. Based on this, I would sell the bonds when the market is crashing. Investing is not a 100% sure thing. These are my recommendations and you need to modify the plan according to your risk tolerance.

13   Using SMA-20 & SMA-50 on stocks

Stocks good for technical analysis

Usually they are large market caps (over one billion) with high volumes. Most of them are optionable and listed in one of the three major stock exchanges. As a riskier alternative, buy options that control more stocks with the same amount of cash. 'Call' options bet the stock to go up and 'put' options bet it to go down; it would help you to remember by thinking of 'calling' up some one and 'putting' down the phone.

Screen for technical indicators

We usually use fundamental screens (P/E, PEG…) to screen stocks and then use technical charts to enter / exit a trade. You can do the opposite: Use technical charts to screen stocks that satisfy some technical indicators such as Head and Shoulder. Use fundamental analysis afterwards on the screened stocks.

Fidelity's Wealth Lab is one with a historical database for their qualified customers.

Finviz.com cam screen stocks using technical indicator. It does not have a historical database for testing. The following YouTube video describes how it is used
https://www.youtube.com/watch?v=RZRP2NeSX0s

Cross over

When the faster SMA-20 (Single Moving Average for the last 20 days) crosses over SMA-50, buy the stock and vice versa. Try SMA-50 and SMA-200 cross over for less frequent trading. There are many other factors in stocks, so do not determine on one indicator/pattern only. Try out the two patterns of a specific stock and see whether it is historically profitable. Again, past performance is no guarantee for future prediction.

Apple as an example

To reduce the number of trades, you can change the days into higher number such as SMA-50 and SMA-200. Experiment the days and the stocks to find the combination that best fits to this strategy. Different stocks react to this cross overs differently.

There are indicators to be considered to ensure the stock is not peaking and overbought (SMA-200% and RSI(14) from Finviz.com). Unless you're using shorts, it is better to select stocks with good fundamentals.

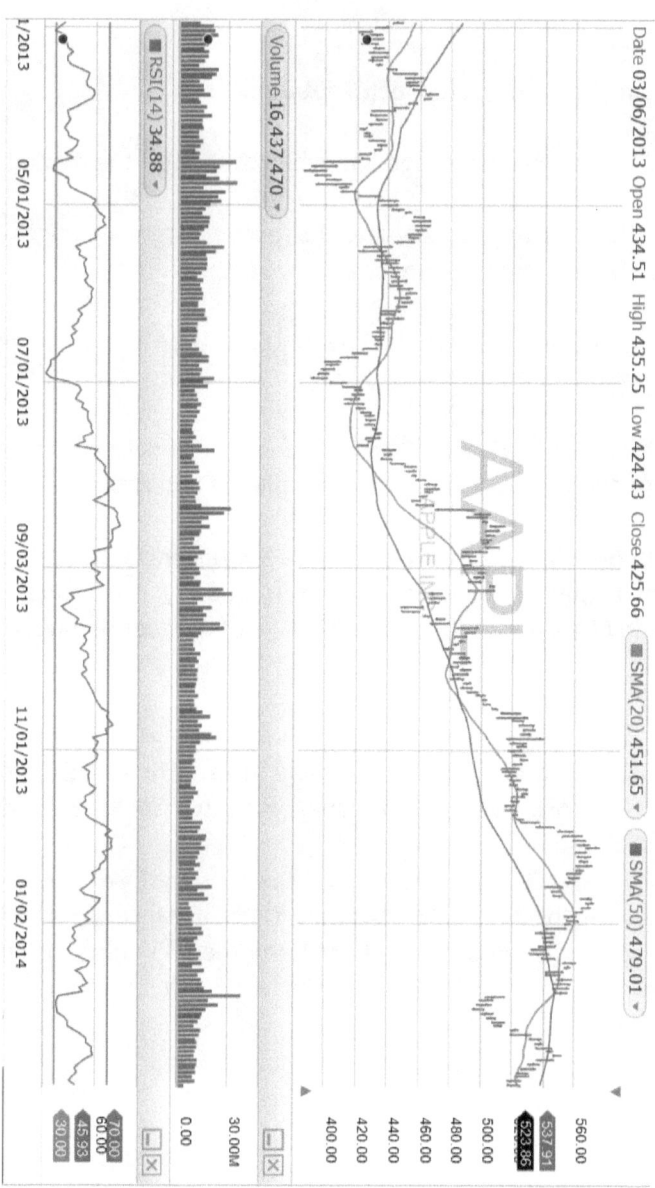

SMA-20 Crosses over SMA-50. Source: Fidelity

14 Using TA for sectors

There are 3 uses of TA for sector rotation.

1. Detect sector plunge and when to reenter the market after plunges.
2. Regular use (usually after its recovery from a plunge).
3. Detect market plunges and/or sector plunges.

#3 has been described on the chapter Spotting Market Plunges and it will not be repeated here.

The difference in #1 and #2 is in the number of days in SMA (Single Moving Average). Use 350 for sector plunge and reentry.

Use 30, 60, 90 or 120 for regular use (i.e. after the reentry from a market plunge) depending on how frequently you rotate. If you rotate in 60 days, use 60 for the average of number of days.

Exit / Reenter a sector ETF

To illustrate, the following example uses XHB (an ETF for the housing sector). Use the same chart for other sector ETFs such as VGK for Europe.

Produce the following chart by using Yahoo!Finance. Enter XHB and select Interactive Chart. Select SMA and then 350 days. Select Max for 'From'.

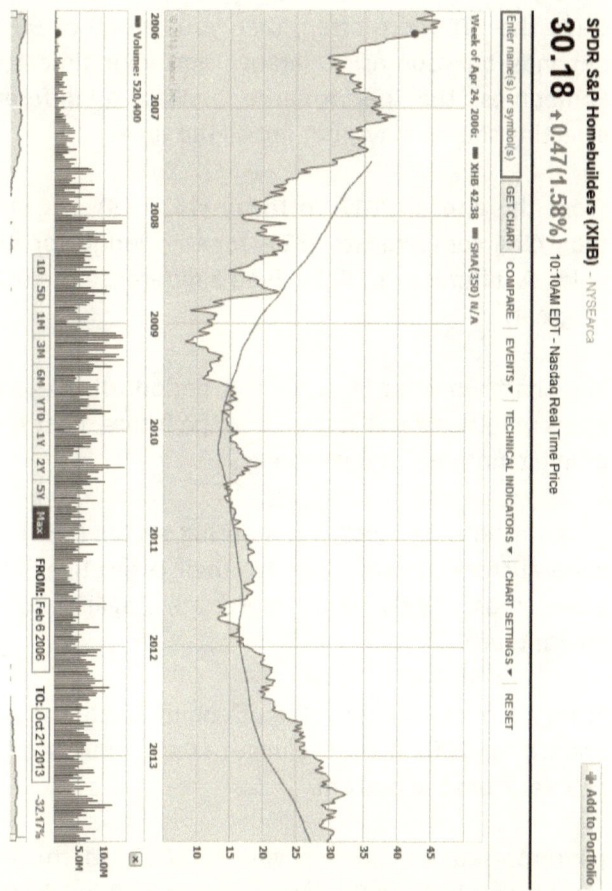

Source: Yahoo!Finance. XHB on 350 SMA.

- Exit when the price falls below the red, single-moving average (the SMA) and enter when it is over the SMA. All the dates and prices are approximate and for illustration only.

- I use Max for the period. Let's assume the chart instructed us to exit at $45 around 2006 and reenter on August, 2009 missing a loss of about $30 per share. Not too bad!

- There are brief exits and reentries before 2012. I call it noises. The gains and losses are negligible. However, make sure you exit and also reenter. If you use 60 days instead of 350 days in this example, you have more noises. If you trade the ETF more often, then you use 60 or 90 days. It depends on your risk tolerance and your time to trade. Sometimes the performance makes a difference in selecting shorter days, but not all the time.

- From the end of 2012 to today (10-2013), it gains more than 40% compared to -32% for the period for buy-and-hold. A difference of 62%! Even a difference of 10% would be great.

- The chart works at least for this period. It is every one's guess whether it will still work in the future. I bet it will but as in life nothing is guaranteed.

- When a housing stock, the housing sector (XHB) and the general stock market all above their respective SMAs, the stock most likely will appreciate (again nothing is guaranteed).

- From my other chapters, the offending sector (housing and finance for 2007 market plunge) takes about two years to recover from the bottom.

  I interpreted the bottom was 10-2007, so the recovery would start in 10-2009. If you bought XHB in 10-2009, you would have gained about 100% today (10-22-2013).

- Some sectors never recover such as the internet and some high tech companies in 2000.

Now, it is your turn to try out the chart. This time, use 60 for the number of days in SMA.

15 Fundamentals vs. Charts

Fundamentalists and chartists debate forever who are on top. Both will make good money if they're good in their respective discipline.

The one who can master the two fields and integrate them will make even more profits at lesser risk. S/he finds stocks using fundamental screens and time the trade (enter / exit) using technical analysis.

Today, you can screen stocks using technical indicators (Finviz.com among one of many sites), and then perform fundamental analysis.

I compare the two techniques in the following table. The data are assigned arbitrarily for discussion.

	Fundamental	Technical analysis
Max. holding period	6 months and analyze again	3 months
Max. no. of stocks	50	15
Best to detect	Bottom	Trend
Irrational market		Better
Min. Research time / stock	One hour / 6 month	15 minutes / day
Manipulated data	Possible	Can't
Avoid plunges	Poor (use stop loss)	Better
Tax treatment	Favorable for long-term gains (check current tax laws)	Unfavorable

Explanation

Holding period

Fundamentalists (me included) hold the stocks they bought for about 6 months on the average according to my swing strategy as described next. After the 6 months, perform another fundamental analysis again to decide whether you want to sell the stock or keep it for another 6 months.

Fundamentals of a company could have changed in less than 6 months. Valued stocks are swimming against the tide, so it takes longer time for the market to recognize their values.

Chartists hold stocks usually less than 3 months. Day traders normally hold stocks less than a day. Charts usually detect the trends than the bottoms.

No. of Stocks

It depends on the size of your portfolio. I recommend 5 stocks in different sectors for a portfolio less than $50,000 for fundamentalists. ETFs are better used here for a diversified portfolio.

Your portfolio should have fewer than 50. Calculate how many stocks you should hold by dividing the total time available by the time you want to spend on each stock in 6 months.

If you have $10 million dollars, most likely you do not want to own 10 stocks with one million each. Adjust the number according to your personal requirements and risk tolerance.

Chartists look at the stocks every day, so I do not suggest they should keep more than 15 stocks. Hence, rarely millionaires are chartists at least not for their entire portfolios.

Both need to add time on market timing and searching / evaluating stocks to trade. Both chartists and fundamentalists should use market timing (i.e. charts) to detect market plunges, peaks and corrections.

Maintain stocks

Fundamentals could spend at least an hour (only possible with subscription services) for each stock they own every 6 months to research whether they want to sell the stock. Chartists watch the stocks they own at least once every day.

Is the current market favor TA or fundamentals

Roughly speaking, Buffett and his followers represent the fundamental analysis and IBD and its followers represent technical analysis. Check out their performances to see which strategy is better for the current market.

There are many sites that show whether value stocks or growth stocks are more favorable in the current market.

If you have a historical database, compare the performances of the top 50 valued stocks and the top 50 growth stocks for the last 90 days to predict the current favorite.

When the market is not rational, usually the chartists win. Everyone's view on this subject is different.

Filler

Tips

Penny stocks are risky as many do not have information required by SEC and the major exchanges. They are traded over the counter, OTC. They cannot be shorted (and most likely you do not want to do so even it was allowed). Pier 1, Ford, American Airlines and many others were all penny stocks.

Expect one winner for several losers. However, the total profit could outpace the total loss if the strategy is properly implemented.

---

16 Momentum and volatility

Take advantage of the fluctuations and the short-term trends of the market. Volatility and Momentum work opposite to each other. Select the fluctuation (volatility) or short-term trend (momentum) according to the current market conditions.

When we've so many 3% fluctuations and the S&P stays flat, you can take advantage of fluctuations by buying a market ETF at the dips (3% down in this example) and selling at the temporary surges (3% up in this example).

Bollinger Bands supposedly indicates stocks normally trading within the bands (upper and lower). This technical indicator is available in most charts such as Yahoo!Finance. For example, enter SPY for the stock and select the Bollinger Bands. You should see the two bands and the stock price in between. Buy when its price is closer to the lower band and sell when it is closer to the higher band.

Momentum is profitable by buying when the last n days is up by x% (you define your n and x and adjust it for the past data). You need to protect your portfolio with stops as momentum can reverse and/or dips can happen unexpectedly. Do the opposite (via a contra ETF) when momentum goes in the opposite direction.

Design tests using historical data from Yahoo!Finance and implement your strategy accordingly. It can also be used to test the direction of the current market. A lot of time volatility happens for a very long period before the market changes direction.

Momentum works better in a rising market. Monitor whether the market peak is close, as it could plunge very fast and very steep. In this case use stop orders to limit big losses due to market plunge.

Links
Volatility:
http://en.wikipedia.org/wiki/Volatility_%28finance%29

Momentum:
http://en.wikipedia.org/wiki/Momentum_%28finance%29

17   How to determine a reversal

This article describes two basic ways to detect a reversal of trend. For illustration purposes, I describe the reversal of an uptrend. The reversal of a downtrend follows similar logic. Volume is the confirmation. Detecting reversal is a technique and it does not always work. Hence, use stops to protect your portfolio and review the stops every week or two for rising stocks.

Simple method

When the SMA-20 (from Finviz.com) drops below SMA-50, it is an indication that the uptrend could be over. For a longer holding period, it is the SMA-50 dropping below SMA-200. If both SMA-20 and SMA-50 are negative, most likely the uptrend turns to a downtrend. You can confirm it with volume; a low volume is not a confirmation.

If it is vastly overbought (RSI(14) > 65) and the volume is low, it could mean that there are no buyers for the ETF. If the peak has occurred, do not be the last one holding that ETF.

ETFs and stocks are normally traded in a range between the resistance and the support. However, when the trend is up and the volume is high, the chance of breaking up the resistance is high. The opposite applies: When the trend is down and the volume is high, the chance of breaking up the support is high.

Complicated method

Method 1. Head and Shoulder is a reliable chart pattern to predict a trend reversal. Basically the uptrend is running out of momentum and hence the reversal (i.e. downturn) is possible. The head indicates a price peak and followed by a smaller peak.

Method 2. A Candlestick charts tell more about an ETF's or stock's movement. Basically it shows the opening price, the closing price and the price fluctuations for the day (or the week if selected). The white body means it is an up day while the black body indicates a down day.

When the candle stick is black (meaning a down day) and is larger than the previous day which is white, it could indicate the uptrend is reversing. The technical term is <u>engulfed candlestick</u>.

When the candle stick returns back to an uptrend, it means the trend is still up and the engulfed candle stick on the second day is a false indicator. It involves 3 candle sticks. It is a more complicated topic.

18   Determine the exit point

I have described 2 exit strategies: Death Cross and SMA-350 (or SMA-400 for fewer false alarms). This is a bonus technique used stand alone or together with the above two. The concept is simple, but it requires more understanding on the charting and candlestick. All the three techniques can be applied to individual stocks, sectors and the market. We demonstrate it with the market using SPY, and the reentry point is just the opposite.

All the three techniques do not identify the top and the bottom as they are based on past data. However, it tells you to exit to avoid further losses. All three have false alarms, but this one could exit earlier. We can tune all the techniques to have fewer false alarms, but it would increase more losses than the original techniques.

The institutional investors (mutual funds, pension funds, etc.) move the market. That's why the volume is important. Whenever there is high volume, most likely they are trading seriously. They may want to make the market rosier than it really is by buying, but the volume is small. When they sell a lot, most likely the market will be down for a while. The following signals that the institutional investors are selling with the exception of the option expiration dates (the Friday of the third week in March, June, September and December):

- Today's trade session is unprofitable.
- The last trade session was unprofitable or had a very tiny profit.
- The trade volume is higher than the trade volume of the last trade session; candlesticks and trade volume are available from most charts.
- The trade volume is higher than the average trade volume of the last 50 trade sessions (available from most charts).
- If the above happens more often (such as 4 times in the last month), be careful. Due to the huge number of stocks the institutional

- investors own, they cannot sell them fast; I estimate it takes about 2 to 4 weeks to dump the stocks.
- The market falls for no reason; the only logical reason could be the institutional investors are dumping.
- Big fall before the market open and it continues for the entire trade day. It indicates many smart moneys including the retail investors are moving out of the market.
- Most likely, Death Cross and SMA-350 (or SMA-400) would signal a down market. SMA-200 would give you a signal ahead of the described two. Using SMA-50 and SMA-200:
  https://www.youtube.com/watch?v=BaZxE12cZP4&t=218s
  https://www.youtube.com/watch?v=wMxj6iB92ZA

The deterioration of the Buy/Sell could indicate the market is falling earlier.

Filler: Black swan

No EU countries want the war in Ukraine for their own benefits. No politicians, even comedians, want to confront an enemy with tanks at the gate. It turns a rich country into the poorest country in the region.

#Filler: health choice

A choice of ice cream and sherbet: one could cause you diabetes and one could cause you heart failure. Both are devilishly delicious.

#Filler: the best health hint

Buy a lottery ticket as early as possible before a big payout. The good feeling of the potential making millions could be the best medicine money can buy.

19 Volume

Most charts show volume of a stock besides its price. Beginners can get daily volume change (Rel. Volume) from finviz.com without charts. It is the confirmation. When the price rises with low volume, it may not indicate the trend is up.

Most stocks rise with breathers. If the stock price rises with high volume and the breathers have low volumes, it confirms an uptrend. If the stock rises with low volume and the breathers have high volume, watch out as the chance of a reversal is high.

Most use daily charts. Weekly charts should be used if the duration holding the stock is longer. The above also applies for stocks trending down.

20 A TA strategy

Buy the stock, sector or the market when: 1. The SMA-50% (from Finviz) is above SMA-200%, 2. SMA-200% is positive, and 3. The price is at least 25% above the 52-week low (i.e., do not buy at the bottom as it may stay there for a long while). Sell, vice versa. Consider other metrics such as Volume, P/E, Debt / Equity, etc. It is great in concept, but I have not been convinced so far in my recent tests.

Related YouTube: Shorter Trend
https://www.youtube.com/watch?v=GAH9EyydEsM
Finding breakout stocks using Finviz.
https://www.youtube.com/watch?v=bWpe30R2VnM
Picking bottom: https://www.youtube.com/watch?v=ygj0TPqmRK4
A TA strategy: https://www.youtube.com/watch?v=ygj0TPqmRK4
Another strategy: CCI + MA
https://school.stockcharts.com/doku.php?id=technical_indicators:commodity_channel_index_cci
https://www.youtube.com/watch?v=CuWzDo72-Rk

Bonus: Market Timing

There is no need to time the market from 1970 to 2000. From 2000 to 2014, the market crashed two times with an average loss of about 45%. Recently, the bull has been long (more than 10 years for the current one) while the bear has been less than 2 years. However, you may gain 10% or so a year in the bull market, while lose 40% or so in the bear market.

Using picking apples as an example, sometimes they may be sour but sometimes they may be tasty. The difference is picking them at the right time. It applies to market timing.

Market timing is about educated guesses. Hopefully we will have more rights than wrongs when we follow general guidelines. It would reduce risk and could benefit us financially in the long run. Recently we have had more false signals than the period between 2000 and 2010. However, it is better to follow a proven system. The harm could be minimal except for tax consequences as the system would tell you to return to the market briefly.

I divide the market timing in three categories by durations as follows. All time durations are estimates for discussion and all markets are different.

	Duration
Secular cycle	20 years (actually less)
Market Cycle	5 years (not the current one)
Correction: 10-20%	1 per year
5-10%	2 per year (count the above as 1)

Market plunges have losses between 30% and 55% usually. There is a gray area for the 20% to 30% losses, which does not happen often. When the market plunges, it plunges hard and fast. The techniques in this book tell you to exit the market and when to return to equities. The techniques are based on falling prices, so they will not indicate peaks and bottoms, but they will help you to reduce further losses.

Within the secular market, there are market cycles. There is a super cycle that I ignore as I find it not too useful. Every market is different. Today we have excessive money printing that changes all the previous logic such as the average length of a market cycle. If the USD is not the reserved currency, the market would fall. However, the correlation of the market and the economy will correlate again. We do not know when, but it will. Otherwise, we have to rewrite all the books on investing. For instant gratification, you can read [Simplest Way to Time the Market](#) and skip the rest of this lengthy section for now.

1   Market timing example

The market is making new highs as of this writing in early 2021. There are always two camps of market timers. One camp predicts a crash is coming while the other predicts it will continue making new highs. This article includes both arguments and suggests how and what actions you need to take to protect your investments. Be warned that all market is different and predictions are just pure predictions; the more educated the guesses, the more chance they will be materialized. In 2021, the market has been flooded with cash due to the excessive printing of money.

Management summary

The market is fundamentally unsound evidenced by fundamental metrics but technically sound evidenced by technical metrics that both will be described in this article. The data were obtained on 09/22/2018. This article shows you how to evaluate the market risk. As of 8/2021, the market has not changed a lot since 01/2020 with the following exceptions: 1.The excessive printing of money that is leading to inflation and 2. The pandemic is still not fully controlled.

Suggested actions
No one predicts the market correctly and consistently. Otherwise, there are no poor folks. Moving the risky investments such as most stocks to cash too early would miss the potential profits. Moving it too late would risk the loss of your stocks.

Your actions depend on your risk tolerance. If you are conservative such as a retiree, you may want to have a larger portion of your investments in lower risk such as CDs and bonds. You can take one of the following three actions or combine all of the three actions.

1. When the market turns to technically unsound, it is time to move your stocks to cash. The market timing indicators may give false signals. In this case, the indicator would tell you to move back to stocks. Most likely you do not lose much except dealing with the consequences of taxes in non-retirement accounts.
2. Move a portion of your risky investments into cash, laddered CDs and/or short-term bonds. Again, the size of the portion depends on your risk tolerance.
3. Use stops. The sell orders would be changed to market orders when the stocks dip below prices specified by you. I prefer to use SPY or other ETF to determine the market direction. Some sectors and some stocks move faster than others. In one crash, my energy stocks were still profitable while the market was tanking. Eventually these energy stocks caught up and fell fast. Today's highly profitable stocks are FAANG stocks as a group.

I propose and prefer 'manual stop orders' to prevent market manipulation. However, usually large ETFs cannot be manipulated easily. Manipulators try to profit from your stop orders. Set a stop order price in your mind. When the stock falls to that specified price, sell it via a market order.

My friend confirmed my "manual stop order":

> "High-frequency trading via Algo Trading Strategy can see exactly where pre-set trailing stops are and sweep across them (play them) like strings on a violin. Pre-set a trailing stop and it is bound to be triggered because Algo hunt them down. Then watch the market rip higher."

Analysis: Fundamentals and Technical

It consists of Fundamental Analysis and Technical Analysis. The former measures how expensive the current market is and the latter measures the trend of the market.

Many metrics were obtained from Finviz.com as of 9/22/2018 while others are obtained from other websites. With the exception of Fidelity.com, all websites described here are free and readily available. It also serves as a guide on how you can do your own market timing especially after a few months.

The following chart uses SPY to represent the market of the top 500 stocks. It is market cap weighted. It means the higher the market cap of the stock, the higher percent of the stock is represented in the index. It turns out most are riskier FAANG stocks. Enter Finviz.com in your browser and enter SPY. I am not responsible for any errors.

Indicator	Pass	Current Value	Indicating
• Technical			
Death Cross[1]		SMA-50 = 2.3% & SMA-200 = 6.3%	Pass
Technical Analysis: 350 SMA%[2]	>0	Price above the SMA-350.	Pass
RSI(14)	<70	61	Pass
Duration (yr.)	<5	10	Fail
		Overall	**Pass**
• Fundamental			
Valuation			
P/E[3]	<15.7	25.4	High by 62%. Fail.
Shiller P/E[3]	<16.6	33.5	High by 102%. Fail
P/B[3]	<2.78	3.52	High by 27%. Fail.
P/S[3]	<1.50	2.33	High by 55%. Fail.
Oil price	30-100	70.71	Pass
Interest rate[6] T-Bill 1 months[7]	<5	2.05	Pass
T-Bill 3 months[7]	Yield	2.18	
T-Bill 30 years[7]	Curve	3.20	Pass
Flow to Equity[4]		-3.371M	Fail
Flow to bond[4]		7.206M	
Corporate debt/GDP[8]	<40	45%	High by 13%. Fail.
USD[5]		Strong	Fail
Gold		High	Fail
Bubble		Several	Fail
Market experts		Fear long term	Neutral
Politics		Trump	Fail
Misc.		Trade war	Fail
		Overall	**Fail**

[1] This is the market timing technique without using a chart.
[2] I tried to use SMA-400% to reduce false signals without success.
[3] Get it from http://www.multpl.com/. Same as CAPE.

[4] Get it from https://www.ici.org/research/stats. It is based on 09-12-18. "Flow to Equity" is based on domestic ETF estimates. Treat it as two phases in moving to equity. First phase of moving excessively to equity indicates the market is peaking. The second phase indicates the market is plunging when the flow of equity is excessively negative.

[5] Global corporations will suffer in profits converted back to USD and hard to sell to foreign countries.

[4] Get it from the above link.

[6] Rising interest is bad for corporations and high-ticket products, but good for lenders.

[7] Get it from https://www.treasury.gov/resource-center/data-chart-center/interest-rates/Pages/TextView.aspx?data=yield based on 09/21/18

[8] With the low interest rate, it may not be that critical. Corporations take advantage of the low interest rate.

Overall

Overall, technical is fine as the market is making new highs. Many aggressive investors exit the market on technical indicators only as the overvalued market could linger on for a long term such as from 2009 to 2017 so far.

Overall, fundamental is not sound. The increasing market price also is decreasing the fundamental metrics such as P/E, P/B and P/S. It is bad unless there is reason to support such as the fast earnings growth in 2009.

Many metrics are deteriorating

RSI(14) is getting closer to 65 (a passing grade specified by me).

Inverse yield curve (1.5 vs. 2.33) is about 61% apart from my interpretation and calculation. It is not a warning now but we should keep an eye on it. Most market crashes have occurred when it is 0% or negative. The theory is that in a normal case the short-term interest rates should be lower than the long-term interest rate.

Another source calculates it is 1.1% and that is very close to inversion since the last recession. From MarketWatch, the 30-year fixed interest rate is 4.66% and 1-year rate is 3.96% giving an inverse yield curve 18% apart, which is quite alarming.

Mathematically incorrect, today's full employment is at 4%. Most recessions are closely preceded by troughs in unemployment and the reverse for the economy to recover.

GDP growth has been predicted from 1.8% to 3%. The 3% is from the White House for their obvious purpose. I predict it will pop up due to meeting the tariff deadlines, tax cuts and spending increases. It will then be declining to 2%. A healthy US economy should maintain 3% without special factors such as excessive immigration.

We have record debts: investors' margin, corporate debt and Federal debt. These are bubbles going to burst. Federal debt / GDP is about [95%](https://fred.stlouisfed.org/series/gfdegdq188S) today. It does not predict the market performance as this ratio was 53% and 55% before the last two market crashes. It will affect the long-term performance of the economy when we have to service the huge national debt.

We do have 10 years of stock growth at the expense of a record Federal deficit. Thanks to President Obama from investors and no thanks from next generations who have to pay back our national debt. It is overdue for a correction. Hopefully it is not a crash which has an average loss of about 45%. We did have two recent corrections losing more than 10%: 2011-12 EU debt crisis and 2014-16 oil crash. The oil price has been rising from $30 per barrel to today's $70. It is still a long way from my warning of $120.

Potential triggers
Trade wars with China, Canada or the EU will be the strongest trigger. Our most profitable companies are virtually all international companies. They need fair trade to prosper.

The other trigger is the possible impeachment of President Trump.

Check the validity of our charts
It seems some metrics vary. It could be used after hour trading. It could be the "Days" may be "Sessions" – calendar day is different

from trading sessions. I selected 10 years for most of the charts and StockCharts let me select only 5 years.

Here is a list of sites for charts.
https://www.stocktrader.com/2013/12/10/best-free-stock-chart-websites/
These are the three sites I use a lot: Fidelity (customers only), StockCharts and Finviz.com (missing some metrics).

As stated before, SPY may not be the best to represent the market. I prefer an ETF for 1,000 stocks and weigh the stocks evenly (i.e., not according to the market cap). Google "market timing 2020 (or current year)" for more expert info. Here is one.

Mid-year update

Basically, nothing significant has changed recently: The market is fundamentally unsound and technically sound after the recent rally. The only update is our national debt is skyrocketing. Today's "Debt/GDP" is similar to the market height in 2000 and we know what happened afterwards. That's why Buffett has accumulated a lot of cash now.

Even with the unlimited QE (i.e., printing money excessively), the high inflation and market crash predicted by many experts have not been materialized so far. This is my third prediction in "Disaster of 2020". The status of USD as a reserve currency will be shaken; I do not know when, as I do not have a time machine.

Why does the market keep going up while the economy is going down? The Fed has provided a lot of cash and the cash is chasing a fixed number of assets such as gold and stocks. It is the simple, proven theory of demand and supply. It will continue for a while as long as there is an unlimited supply of money. At some point, it will pop. At that time, it could lead to a long recession, unless the economy improves as it did in 2009. The smart Fed chairman knows how it will harm the country by excessively printing money. However, he has to obey his boss who is seeking reelection.

I expect we are in a prolonged period of low interest rates and even negative interest rates. When the rates are negative, our Treasury bonds are no longer marketable. The foreign central banks including China would dump our national debts if it has not already started. The economy is dressed up nicely in an election year. Giving us free money is the easy way to buy votes, but the long-term effects are very harmful.

Using cheap money to buy back the company's stock would boost the stock price and hence make the management wealthier. It is a false sense of the stock value. When the company cannot pay back the debt obligations, the company would go bankrupt. If the U.S. were a company, she would have gone bankrupt already.

As of 6/15/2020, QQQ (representing NASDAQ stocks) has been up 11% YTD and it is far better than DIA (representing DOW stocks) and SPY (representing the 500 large stocks in the S&P Index and losing about 5% YTD). QQQ has a lot of tech stocks while DIA has a lot of losers including Boeing. Most FAANG stocks are making record highs and QQQ is market cap weighted.

Most of the ETFs on chips have been up more than 40% in a year. I bought Amazon and two chip ETFs. I use trailing stops to protect my portfolio. Huawei is buying a lot of U.S. chips in the 120-day relaxed period. In September this year and if there is no extension, I would sell these chip ETFs fast.

I have used the strategy described in my book "Profit from the recovery of the pandemic" to take advantage of this volatile market. I used 5% as the threshold and I had too few trades; now I changed to 3%. Expecting a market crash, I weigh more on contra ETFs. As described in the same book, I bought a lot of contra ETFs, GLD and the stock of a gold miner. It is for insurance. Oil ETFs are my big mistake.

If the U.S.D. loses the status of reserve currency (not likely soon), it would bring prolonged depression and high inflation in the U.S. In this case, it is safer to invest in real estate, precious metals and profitable companies than in CDs and bonds that would lose value due to inflation.

Check out many articles on the status of the current market. Many have opposing views, so you have to make your own decision. In any case, play it safe with stops. Here is one article from MarketWatch.com.

Update 8/2021

Nothing has changed. The market is not sound fundamentally but fine technically. When the technical indicators tell us to exit, most likely it is right. However, the market is volatile, and hence return to the market if the indicators tell us so. Here is an argument from opposite camps.
https://www.youtube.com/watch?v=I9P9IuwuTVE

Canary warning?

When I was working on my new book "Best stocks to buy for 2021" on Dec. 10, 2020, I found something really strange. I have never rejected so many stocks that have Fidelity's Equity Summary Score higher than 9. I rejected them as there was a lot of dumping from the insiders. Insiders know their companies better than most of us. Is it the canary telling us the market is overvalued?

Initially the following stocks have been screened by my value screens. Buy any one of the following stocks, **only** if you have good reason(s).

How can HEAR score a perfect 10 while the Insiders' Transaction is -75% (to me -2% is normal). The analysts must be wrong this time, or they believe the market will continuously make new heights.

Symbol	Fidelity Score	Insider Purchase	Return[1]	Annualized
BCC	9.9	-24%	46%	126%
GPI	10.0	-17%	35%	95%
HEAR	10.0	-75%	43%	118%
HVT	9.5	-37%	53%	144%
HZO	9.5	-27%	75%	204%
Average				84%
SPY				30%
Beat SPY[2]				177%

[1] From Dec. 20, 2020 to July 1, 2021. Fees, commissions and dividends are not included.

² = (Average − SPY) /SPY. SPY represents the market to many of us. This concludes the Insiders are wrong in this case.

A correction or a crash?
In Dec., 2018, the S&P 500 is about 15% down and a crash is about 45% down.

If a crash is coming, there should be an additional 30% down. If it is a correction (15% average), then we have it already. Should we pick up bargains now? Or, are they bargains? It is a trillion-dollar question.

We need a trigger for a market crash like the financial crisis in 2008 and the internet bubble in 2000. Besides the record-high margin debt, the possibility of Trump's impeachment and a trade war, I do not see any.

Links
Search articles from Google and YouTube on today's market conditions.
YouTube: 1
https://www.youtube.com/watch?v=czHUI0syjKo&t=300s

Filler: CIA mistook it as a missile silo in China.

2 Simplest market timing

Why market timing

Before 2000, market timing was a waste of time. However, after that, we have had two market plunges with the average loss of about 45%. It sounds harder to time the market than it actually is. We have a simple technique to detect market plunges and when to reenter the market. Our objective is reducing the loss to 25%.

Market timing depends on charts; the following describes how to use chart information without creating charts. Most charts will not identify the peaks and bottoms of the market as they depend on data (i.e., the stock prices). However, it would reduce further losses. It is simpler than it sounds. Just follow the procedure below.

The first part of this technique detects potential market plunges, and the second part advises you when to start reentering the market. It applies to individual stocks too. It also works to detect the trend of a sector (entering an ETF for the specific sector instead of SPY) and a specific stock.

Step-by-step procedure

When the market timer indicator (Death Cross) described next tells you to exit the market, sell SPY (an ETF simulating S&P 500). Do not forget to buy back SPY or similar ETF such as RSP, when the indicator (Golden Cross) tells you to return.

My experiences in 2000s

Basically I did the same as the above with some adaptations. I worked for a mutual fund company and they did not allow me to trade stocks effectively. However, I was allowed to trade sector funds offered by the company. Every two months, I switched to the sectors with the best performances for the last month. When most sectors were down for the last month, I rotated them to the money market fund. In March or April, 2000, I switched to traditional sectors from high-tech sectors (better to switch to market money funds). During that time, I bought stocks that had enough cash to last more than two years judging by their burn rates. The indicators should do a better job.

How to detect market plunges without charts (similar to <u>Death Cross</u>)
1. Bring up Finviz.com.
2. Enter SPY (or any ETF that simulates the market) or RSP, equally-weighted SPY.
3. If SMA-200% is positive, it indicates that the market plunge has not been detected and you can skip the following steps.
4. The market is plunging if SMA-50% is more negative than SMA-200%. To illustrate this condition, SMA-200% is -2% and SMA-50% is -5%.
5. Another hint: B/S (buy sell ratio) is negative, specially it is more negative than last week.
6. Conservative investors should sell most stocks starting with the riskiest ones first such as the ones with negative earnings, high P/Es and/or high Debt/Equity. Obtain this info from Finviz.com by entering the symbol of the stock you own.
7. Aggressive investors should sell all stocks. Extremely aggressive investors should sell all stocks, buy contra ETFs such as PSQ, and even short stocks. I do not recommend beginners to be aggressive.

Example

As of 2/12/2022, the following are from Finviz.com.

ETF	SMA-200	SMA-50	SMA-20	Death Cross?
SPY	-0.8%	-4.2%	-1.7%	Yes (Step #4)
RSP	-0.5%	-1.9%	0.4%	Yes (Step #4)

Both ETFs indicate the market is a confirmed crash from my indications using a technique similar to Death Cross. However, they are quite close, and we should keep an eye on these numbers. In this case, SMA-20 has not been used. If it is a false alarm, the Golden Cross would indicate it and you should return to equity; it could be quite common in volatile markets. The futures indicate that on Monday (2/14/22) the market would plunge further. Another test is using SMA-350: When the current price is below SMA-300, it is a crash. SMA-20 has to be more negative than SMA-50 and it has not been used here.

Simple chart example. Bring up StockCharts.com and enter SPY. It indicates Death Cross occurred on about March 20, 2022.

When to return to the market (similar to Golden Cross)

Use the above in a reversed sense to detect whether the market has been recovering. However, when the SMA-200% turns positive, I would start buying value stocks (low P/E but the 'E' has to be positive, and/or low Debt/Equity).

1. Bring up Finviz.com.
2. Enter SPY (or any ETF that simulates the market).
3. If SMA-200% is negative, the market is not recovering, and you can skip the following steps.
4. Sell all contra ETFs and close all shorts if you have any.
5. Market recovery is confirmed when SMA-50% is more positive than SMA-200%. To illustrate this condition, SMA-200% is 2% and SMA-50% is 5%. Commit a large percent of cash (or all cash for aggressive investors) to stocks. If you do not know what to buy, buy SPY or an ETF that simulates the market.
6. Another hint: B/S (buy sell ratio) is positive, specially it is more positive than last week.

How often should you check the market timing indicators?

Do the above once a month. When the SPY price is closer to SMA actions percentage, perform the above once a week. The charts and data for market timing described in this book are based on SMA-350 (Simple Moving Average) that is more preferable than this simple procedure, but it requires some simple charting.

Nothing is perfect

If the market timing is perfect, there would be no poor folks. The major 'defects' are:
- It does not detect the peak / bottom as it depends on past data. However, it would save you a lot during the crash.
- It is hard to determine whether it is a correction or a crash.
- From 2000 to 2010, there was only one false signal. The indicator tells you to exit and then tells you to reenter the market shortly. In most cases, you do not lose a lot. After 2010, we have more false signals.
- The market may not be rational or may be influenced due to specific conditions such as excessive printing of USD. If you do not mind charting, use SMA 350 (or 400) using SPY. Buy when the price is above SMA-350 (or SMA-400), and sell otherwise. SMA-400 reduces the number of false signals, but it is not nimble.
- I do not recommend Bitcoin but agree with most of thinking of this YouTube.
  https://www.youtube.com/watch?v=a5J8gMrEZxg

3   Why the market fluctuates

The following chart uses SPY (simulating the market) with SMA-350 for the year of 2020 using Fidelity's charting function. It will be used to demonstrate how SMA-350 worked for 2020; the dates may be several days off. This article is written on 1/1/2021.

Market Timing
SMA-350 (Simple Moving Average for the last 350 sessions), described in this book, worked fine in 2020. It told us to exit the market on about 3/11/2020 and return on about the beginning of June. There were two false signals (on about 4/28 and 5/8) that told you to exit but return to the market shortly.

The other indicators are RSI(14) and P/E. Fidelity's chart uses 80 for overbought and 30 for under-bought for RSI(14). The market has been overpriced for a long while. In this case, technical analysis (SMA-350 I used in my example) works better than fundamental (P/E as one of the metrics); It has been sold for the entire 2020.

Why there is a big drop in late March and why it comes back
The trigger is the pandemic.

The market came back for many reasons:
- We understood the pandemic better.
- A lot of money on the sideline.
- The government supplies more money by printing it excessively.
- The government lowers the interest rate (almost to zero).

2021 prediction
It is quite hard to predict the market. Here are my thoughts. The market is not rational (fundamentally speaking).

For:
- The government keeps on excessively supplying money.
- With easy credit, the rising housing market leads to many profitable sectors such as furniture.
- Due to easy credit and recovery, many companies buy back their own stocks.
- Low margin interest rate usually boosts the stock market.
- If the vaccines can control this pandemic, many sectors will recover. As I demonstrated before, we have to wait one more year for some sectors such as airlines, restaurants and cruise lines.
- Trade war with China could be reduced under Biden.

Against:
- The pandemic has not been stopped.
- Unemployment is breaking the previous record.
- Small businesses continue to go bankrupt.
- Complete decoupling with China.
- The government tools do not work anymore such as lowering interest rate.
- Super inflation is due to ample supply of money chasing a fixed amount of assets (stocks for example). It would also shake the status of the USD as a reserve currency.

As in any market, there are two camps opposite to each other. Need to watch the market like a hawk and take actions accordingly (talk to your financial advisor first). I expect the plunge would cause the market to lose about 40% if it happens.

4   Market cycle

"Bull markets are born on pessimism, grow on skepticism, mature on optimism, and die on euphoria" - Sir John Templeton

The stock market has cycles as our practical interpretation of the above. It is about five years apart, but it fluctuates widely. I divide it into four stages: Bottom, Early Recovery, Up and Peak.

My defined four stages of a market cycle

We need to apply the right investing strategies to each of the four stages of the cycle.

- **Bottom**

    I would not invest for at least the first six months (or even a year) after the big plunge starts, which could lose over 25% in a few months. The exceptions are investing in contra ETFs and selling short for aggressive investors.

    I estimate it will take a year from the start of the plunge to the bottom, so I will normally sell stocks early in the plunge and do not buy stocks that are in the sector (sometimes sectors) that cause the bubble for about two years after the plunge.

    At the bottom, the high-yield corporate bonds (i.e., junk bonds) would prosper when the interest rate is decreasing to stimulate the economy.

    From mid-2007 to mid-2008, bonds suffered as the investors thought the sky was falling down - it was to those who lost their jobs and/or their houses. After that, some bonds, especially the long-term bonds, could appreciate about 50% in the following year.

    The government lowered the interest rates and these bond prices with high interest rates surged. Correct timing in buying bonds could be very profitable.

Long-term bonds have more impact by the interest rate: The lower the interest rate, the higher the bond prices of higher-yield bonds. The older bonds with higher interest rates are more valuable to the newer bonds with lower interest rates.

I define this period of the bottom from the start of the plunge to the start of Early Recovery.

- **Early Recovery**
It usually starts after one year from the plunge; no one can pinpoint the exact time consistently. By this time preferably earlier, we should have closed out all positions in contra ETFs and shorts.

Roughly speaking, October, 2007 (some use 2008) is the start of the market plunge. March, 2009 is the end of the bottom stage and the start of the early recovery stage of the 2007 cycle. However, every market cycle is different in where it starts and ends.

The one-year gain from the bottom is most profitable. It usually gains over 25% in a year from the market bottom. I, a conservative investor, had huge gains using some leverage in my largest taxable account in 2009. From my memory, I had a similar return in 2003 but I had not saved the statement as in 2009.

In this phase, value is a better parameter than growth in searching for stocks. If your investment subscription provides a composite value score and a composite timing score, the sort parameter of your screened stocks could be "Composite Value / Composite Timing" in descending order. Select the top stocks in this order. You still have to analyze the top-screened stocks.

Forward (same as Expected) P/E is a good metric. However, most companies may be losing money at this stage. Those companies that can last for more than one year with its cash reserve are potential good buys. The best appreciated stocks are beaten companies that have precious technologies and good customer bases. They could be candidates to be acquired if they are small enough.

- **Up**
  Usually, the growth metrics such as PEG could be better than the value metrics such as expected P/E during this phase. Most stocks are winners except contra ETFs and shorting stocks. When the growth stocks are making headlines and the defensive stocks are being dumped, this is the hint that we're well into the Up phase of the market cycle.

  Locate stocks with growth metrics such as favorable PEG and high SMA-200% (from Finviz.com). Do not be scared of how much they have already appreciated. The strategy "Buy High and Sell Higher" works in this phase. Protect your profits with stops.

  Ensure that they have value too. Skip the stocks with expected P/Es higher than 35 unless there are good reasons. Most stocks will gain due to the tide of the market. However, when they're overbought (RSI(14) over 65), be careful. When institutional investors sell these stocks, they will crash.

- **Peak**
  When everyone makes easy money and the interest rates are high, watch out. Stop loss and/or stop limit should be used to protect your investment. Check out whether there is any bubble that would burst like the internet in 2000 and finance (and housing) in 2007.

  The internet crisis is easy to spot, but not the financial crisis. In 2007 we had a cycle longer than the average which is about 5 years. The plunge is very fast and very steep – thanks to the institutional investors who drive the market down.

  Run the technical analysis chart described in the Chapter on Spotting Big Market Plunges at least monthly (weekly if you have time). Protect your investment. Do not fall in love with any stock (you can buy it back later at a deep discount). Making the last buck is a fool's game.

Accumulate cash according to your risk tolerance. A retiree or a conservative investor would accumulate from 25% to 50% and should be ready to move to all cash when the plunge starts.

We can lower the cash percent if we use enough stop loss protection. Be psychologically prepared because the stock market may still rise for a while. There is no perfect market timing.

The 2007 Cycle
The market plunged starting in 10-2007 and ending in 3-2009 (bottom), started to recover in 3-2009 (early recovery), and trended up from 2010 to 1-2013 (the up phase of the market cycle). As of 3/2016, it is the peak phase defined by me.

As of 1/2013, we have recovered all the market losses since 2007. However, as of 7/2014, the economy has not fully recovered compared to the economy before the plunge. The employment judging by the medium salary has not fully recovered and the economy is not expanding. It is uncommon that the economy does not follow the market. It is due to the excessive supply of money by the government and partly due to globalization to allow companies to hire overseas.

Although a W-shaped recession seldom happens, we have a chance today. We hope we do not have a depression and/or the similar lost decades that Japan has been experiencing. Some may conclude we are close to completing a market cycle from 2007 to 2016. As of 2016, the economy is recovering slowly and we're better than most other global economies.

Again, market timing is not an exact science as it involves irrational human beings and government interventions. The timing using the market cycle described here is a guideline as it is hard to time it exactly.

The average market cycle is about 5 years, but they fluctuate. If we consider 2007 as the plunge, we have about 8 years of this cycle as of 2015.

In a typical cycle (few are typical), we have about one year in each of the 4 phases I defined (plunge, early recovery, up and peak).

Events/Triggers

There are financial events and triggers that cause the transition of one phase of the market cycle to another. They usually do not change the sequence of the phases (say not from Peak to Early Recovery), but they may change the duration of the phase. Examples are:

- The government announcing change of the interest rate,
- Change of employment, and
- Change of GNP.

Sectors in a market cycle (my suggestion)

Market Phase	Favorable	Unfavorable
Early Recovery	Financial, Technology, Industrial	Energy, Telecom, Utilities
Up	Technology, Industrial, Housing	
Peak	Mineral, Health Care, Energy, Long-Term Bond, Consumer Discretionary	
Bottom	Consumer Staples, Utilities	Consumer Discretionary, Technology, Industrial, Long-Term & high-yield Bond

The sectors that cause the recession usually take a longer time to recover. In 2000, the technology sector was not favorable in the Early Recovery phase, contrary to the above table. In 2007, the financial sector was not favorable in the Early Recovery phase. These are the "offending" sectors that cause the plunges.

In a recession, we usually cannot cut down on consumer staples and utilities, but we can cut down on buying consumer gadgets. Companies usually postpone investing in equipment and systems during a recession and expand when the economy is humming. The government usually lowers the interest rates right after the plunge to stimulate the economy.

Conclusion

When the market is about to plunge or change from one stage to another, run the described chart more frequently and read more articles written by the experts.

Again, market timing is not an exact science but it is based on educated guesses. The better guesses should have more rights than wrongs in the long term. Our actions depend on our risk tolerance. Be careful of using any new strategy that has not been fully understood and proven. Since 2000, market timing is very important to your financial health with two market plunges with an average of about 45% loss.

Afterthoughts

- The Dow Theory has a lot of followers in detecting market directions. In a nutshell, the market heading upwards is confirmed by the Industrial Index and the Transportation Index (less important in today's market especially with internet sales such as songs and movies), and vice versa. As of 4/2014, the two indexes are not in uniform.
  http://finance.yahoo.com/blogs/talking-numbers/this-is-a-130-year-old-warning-sign-for-stocks-231901097.html
- The bear market has the following three phases.
1. The market is overvalued.
2. Corporations are not doing well with decreasing earnings and sales.
3. Investors are selling due to fears.

It is the reverse for a bull market: 1.The market is under-valued. 2. The market increases due to increasing corporate profits/sales and 3. Investors are buying due to greed.

- Investopedia has several articles on this topic.
  http://www.investopedia.com/terms/b/businesscycle.asp

- The yield curve could predict the interest rates change and hence the economy. There are three main types of yield curve shapes: normal, flat and inverted.

A normal yield curve is one in which longer maturity bonds have a higher yield. Similarly, the long-term CD should have a higher interest rate than the short-term CD.

When the shorter-term yields are higher than the longer-term yields, it indicates an upcoming recession. A flat yield curve indicates the economy is transiting. Now, you've read the essence of a book on this topic costing about $50 to buy.

However, especially today, it does not mean anything as the government supplies too much money to stimulate the economy unsuccessfully. My simple chart described using SMA-350 (Simple Moving Average for 350 trading sessions) which depends on the stock price works better. Click here for "The dynamic yield curve" (http://stockcharts.com/freecharts/yieldcurve.php).

The interest rate plays a role too. The easy money encourages folks to borrow money to buy stocks and companies to acquire other companies.

- As of Feb., 2013, I believe we're in the Up stage of the market cycle. I checked the performances of my top screens from each stage (a.k.a. phase) of the market cycle for the last 60 days. The best performance as a group belongs to the screens for the Up stage. Controversial! Always use the screens (same as searches) that perform well recently.

In addition, the market has recovered 120% of the loss of 2007-2008. Hence the duration for an average Up stage of the market is quite close.

- Total Market Cap / GNP ratio is hotly debated on the market value. Different from the traditional 100%, I would suggest that the boundary ratio should be 130%. If it is over 130%, the market is overvalued and vice versa.
http://www.investopedia.com/terms/m/marketcapgdp.asp

Market cycle:
https://www.youtube.com/watch?v=ebWL2TrIssA

5 Market timing by calendar

The following predictions are based on historical data. You may have slightly different findings depending on when you start and when you end your testing.

You can load the historical data of SPY via Yahoo!Finance and check out how close you are or different from my own predictions. They are my predictions based on historical data. Use it as a reference only.

- <u>Presidential cycle.</u>
  Usually, the market performs worse in the first two years after the election than the next two. During the **3rd year** the president has to make the economy look rosy in order to buy votes. Statistically it is the best year for the market and is followed by a good year (the election year). The government may stimulate the economy, the stock market and employment by printing more money, lowering interest rates and lowering taxes. The market in the 100 days before the election should be positive and less volatile according to 40 years of data. The next 100 days after the inauguration should be good for the market (termed as the honeymoon period).

  Democratic presidents have better market performance statistically than Republican presidents. This is not too logical as though Republicans are more pro-business traditionally.

- Olympics.
  It has been proven that the host country has a better chance that its stock market appreciates the year after the Olympics. It could be due to the exposure from the Olympics and / or the huge expenses in preparing for the Olympics.

  The last two Olympics follow this pattern as of 12/23/2013:

Olympics Country / Year	ETF	Period	Return
United Kingdom / 2012	EWU	Jan. 3, 2013 - Dec. 23,2013	11%
China / 2008	FXI	Jan. 3, 2009 - Dec. 31, 2009	43%

Greece could be an exception. It is too small a country to host this world-class event and it has wasted too many resources by building too many white elephants that the country can never justify. Brazil depends on its export of natural resources to China, so I do not count on the Olympics effect there. Japan 2020 was adversely affected by the pandemic.

Winning a lot of Olympic medals has no prediction for the stock markets. Both the Russian Empire and E. Germany were winners but disappeared in their original forms afterwards.

- Seasonal.
  Best profitable investment period is: Nov. 1 to April 30 of the following year. It is similar to the saying 'Sell in May and Go away'. It has not worked since 2009 as it was an Early Recovery (defined by me) in the market cycle.

  The market does not always happen as predicted. However, when more folks follow this, it becomes a self-fulfilling prophecy. I prefer "Sell on April 15 and come back on Oct. 15" to act before the herd. The more practical strategy is to start selling on April 1 and become more aggressive (selling at closer to the market prices) when it is close to May 1. For the last five years, I did not find this prediction reliable.

  The explanation of the 'summer doldrums' could be that the investors cash their stocks for vacations and college tuition in the fall. Buying quality companies at the dips could be profitable.

- The worst month: September.
  The next worst month is October. However, if there is no serious market crash during October (and this month has more than its shares of crashes), it could be the best month to buy stocks.

- The best month for the bull: November.
  However, several market bottoms occurred in October and November. The next strong month is December. Most experts believe the best 3 months of the year starts in November.

- Best 30 days: Dec. 15 to Jan. 15, next year.
  It was correct for the period of 2012-2013.

- Window dressing.
  Institutional investors sell their losers and buy winners around Nov. 1. From my rough estimate and on the average, the winners have a 2% percentage point gain better than the market and the losers have 1% worse than the market.

  I recommend that you evaluate the top 10 winners from the last 10 months or YTD on Oct. 15 and sell them at 3% gain or two months later.

  I recommend that you buy in Dec. and sell them 3 months later. Include the stocks with more than 30% loss for the last 11 months or YTD, sort them by Earning Yield in descending order and evaluate the top 10 stocks.

  In both cases, do not buy foreign stocks and stocks with return of capital. Ignore stocks not in the three major exchanges, with low volumes and stock prices less than $2. Do not buy in losing years such as 2007 and 2008. I have my tests with my own assumptions and I use tools not available to most readers. From my own experiences, I made more money by buying the losers from Dec. 15 to end of Dec. than buying the window dressers.

This is a guideline only. Do not buy any stocks during market plunges. Current events should be considered first such as a potential war and the hiking of interest rates.

Afterthoughts

- I predict it will be a sideways market in the later part of 2013. I am following the sideways strategy: Buy on dips and sell when the market is up. One's prediction.

- Why September has a bad reputation?
  http://www.marketwatch.com/story/betting-on-septembers-terrible-odds-2013-08-27?dist=beforebell

September of 2013 (2 days away at the time of this writing) may have more problems. Check out how many of the following are correct on Oc. 1, 2013. Use it as a future guideline to predict the next September using the current market conditions then:

1. The market is not excessively expensive, but it is not cheap. It is due for a 5% correction.
2. Unrest in Syria (check any unrest in your next prediction in September).
3. High oil prices due to Syria.
4. September is statistically a bad month for the stock market. However, it could be an opportunity to invest after the correction if any.
5. Interest rates are rising.
6. All the above indicate the market will dip. However, the rosier outlook is that the global economies are improving even slowly.

- January effect.
  The performance of January may determine how the entire year performs. I cannot find any rationale but it has been proven right statistically.

- Earnings period announced in Jan., April, July and Oct. would cause big swings in stocks when they have surprises. Earning revisions could be a good predictor.
  http://www.investopedia.com/terms/e/earningsseason.asp

Links
Presidential Cycle:
http://www.investopedia.com/articles/financial-theory/08/presidential-election-cycle.asp
Calendar-based market timing:
http://stock-chartist.com/2010/10/calendar-based-market-timing/
Calendar market timing for 2013:
http://www.investorecho.com/archives/8047

6   Profitable Early Recovery

I had an 80% return in 2009 in my largest taxable account. I did not include it in my other books before as I just found the statement. Early Recovery, a phase of the market cycle defined by me, is the best time to make a profit. My chart told me to start to move to equity in September, 2009. I did in March, 2009 for other reasons. It could be luck, technique or both.

I did dip into the credit line of my equity loan (not recommended to most) due to lower interest rates than a margin interest. I paid back the loan right after I sold some stocks. The turnaround was high until I exhausted my short-term losses (tax loss harvest). The strategy is bottom fishing. Some sectors described are better in this stage of the market cycle.

I had similar success in 2003. I did not have a defined bottom fishing technique at that time. I expected the market to fully recover in two years. From Value Line, I selected stocks with high "Projected 3-5 year returns" and the short-term assets can last for two more years (judged by the burnt rates).

As the stocks are recovering earnings (E), the trailing P/E may not be a good indicator, but the Forward P/E may be. Most sites on evaluating stocks such as Fidelity have a value grade. Also look for candidates for acquisition. From the last recoveries, I spotted at least one such candidate. They are usually small companies (50 to 300M market cap) and have valuable assets such as customer base and patents. Aggressive investors should buy stocks with the worst timing grades and this the only time to do so; these beaten-up stocks could be big winners.

An article stated that the entire company of an internet company can fit into the conference room of Exxon, and it had the same market cap as Exxon if my memory serves me right. In early April, 2000, I switched all my tech mutual funds in my annuity into traditional sectors (better to cash in hindsight) to avoid the crash. Fishing in the market bottom is risky but very profitable. The Golden Cross could miss the bottom as it depends on past data. Other hints are Buy / Sell ratio is less than 0.2, RSI(14) for SPY is less than 25 and the market has more than 40% lower from the peak.

The stocks that have been beaten down badly and have poor timing scores could be the stocks that have the highest appreciation potential. It is different from the traditional evaluation. I prefer those stocks with positive earnings or at least not losing a lot. The appreciation periods for most of these stocks may not last long. Hence, I recommend using trailing stops (and reviewing the stops periodically) for appreciating stocks. To illustrate, you do not want to lose more than 10% from the peak of a stock and do not take profit prematurely.

My predictions for 2023. If the market recovers in 2023, it could be the beginning of a new cycle. We can use the market timing indicator to confirm it. If there is a serious recession, all bets would be off.

I invested a lot of defensive stocks such as consumer staples, healthcare and utilities. The stocks I recommended in 79% or my book "Best stocks for 2022" has a return of 4% beating RSP by 153% from Dec. 15, 2021 to Dec. 1, 2022. Not counting market timing and the acquired USAK that gained 79% and annualized to 105%.
http://tonyp4idea.blogspot.com/2022/12/best-stocks-series.html

During market recovery, usually the beat-up stocks recover first. Usually the small stocks gain larger profit in the short term and then the large caps. Ensure the stocks are profitable or at least Forward P/E is positive.

Links:
Bottom fishing:
https://www.youtube.com/watch?v=hANAn9szRBA
Recommended stocks for Q3 2022. Understand why.
https://www.youtube.com/watch?v=4IxS7pfGukM

7   Market timing of 2022

As of this writing (2/2023), fundamentals of the market had been poor for the past few years, but the market had been rising until 2022. It confirms again that technical analysis is more important than fundamentals in market timing. Our simplest technical analysis that does not require charting told us to leave the market in March, 2022. Most of us did not follow it – I am guilty as charged. We should at least move some of the risky stocks such as the FAANG stocks to cash.

All markets are different. The fast recovery of the 2008's market is due to China's purchase of a lot of our debts at the request of the chairman of the Federal Reserve Bank. Now we treat China as our enemy and China is having their own financial problems, and hence they will not help us again. Many 'experts' expected the market would not recover even in 2015.

The culprit of our market has been printing too much money. It is the trick of buying votes, especially during Trump and now Biden's eras. Our national debt is about 129% to GDP in 2022. Our government spending seems to be limitless, as they do not know how to fix our problems.

The government has given out a lot of money to our citizens. Many low-wage workers do not work with free money. It leads to hyperinflation (as high as 9.1% at one time in 2022). The government is forced to hike interest rates to fight inflation, and in turn it leads to a poor economic outlook. Consequently, the bubble of the booming house market (also affecting many companies selling big-ticket items) would burst in 2023. The high-tech companies suffer most as we do not need to upgrade our iPhones or buy any gadgets. Those companies depending on advertising such as Facebook and YouTube suffer too. Many high-tech companies are laying off high-salary employees. The only bright area is AI with the amazing ChatGDT that would affect many companies including NVDA producing AI chips.

Use the Golden Cross in the described market timing in this book to re-enter the market slowly and gradually. Personally I am looking for fundamentally sound companies that will prosper in the future. Again, consult your financial planner before taking any actions.

Links

How the market works: https://www.youtube.com/watch?v=IsM0huAyyw0

Epilogue

After my early retirement, I have been spending most of my time in investing, running thousands of simulation and reading over one hundred books in investing. Starting from 2000, I have been doing extraordinary good. I comment in financial blogs and save the good ones in my own blog, so I can refer them later on. After several years, I have enough information to write a book.

At first, I want to write a book for one reader only: Me. My children have better things to do than investing. I do not need to keep my 'secrets' for them. That's why I publish this book. From the version before its release, it had been doing better than my expectation. It has been very rewarding, when my readers tell me how much they enjoy and benefit from this book.

It is far more financially rewarding working on my investment including finding new strategies. Writing books and articles takes time away from my investing and it actually costs me more money. However, it has been fun to write this book and to interact with my readers. Money cannot buy everything.

I do not believe that this book or any book is the Holy Grail in investing. However, it has a lot of fresh ideas and good pointers that have brought me financial success (at least so far). I ask my readers to challenge my pointers and ensure they are applicable in today's market and meet their objectives and requirements.

A good pointer can make you thousands of dollars, and a bad or misinterpreted one can do the opposite. Always do paper trading on any strategy and / or idea before you commit real money on it. Start your strategy with cash in small increments until you have more confidence.

If you believe this book is beneficial, please comment in amazon.com or similar sites.

Appendix 1 – All my books

Book	No. of Pages	Link	ebook	Rating /5
Art of investing 5th Edition	590	Click here	link	4.5
Sector Rotation: 21 strategies 5th Edition	500	Click here	Link	9.5/10
Be a stock expert in 5 minutes. Expanded Edition.	203	Click here	Link	
Using Finviz 5th Edition	600	Click here	Link	4.5
Using Fidelity 5th Edition	600	Click here	Link	4.5
Momentum Investing 3rd Edition	285	Click here	Link	
Using profitable investing sites	520	Click here	link	
Investing successes and plunders	410	Click here	Link	
Best stocks to buy for 2025	375	Click here	Link	
Profit from bull, bear and sideway market	240	See ebook	Link	4
Artificial intelligence investing	420	See ebook	Link	
Profitable covered call	615		Link	4
Your best dollar for smart investing. $1 all the time.	65		Link	4

The ratings are usually done by ChatGPT and/or DeepSeek (AI) which

the most unbiased.

If you already have my book that is over 400 pages, most likely you do not need to buy the above books except "Investing successes and plunders" and the "Best Stock" series, which may be available every December with the title such as "Best stocks for 2026" – not a promise.

For paper-bag readers, access the links via the following link. https://www.blogger.com/blog/post/edit/7608574268453692676/1786802320953936467

Full AI reviews on my books and articles: TonyP4Idea: Summary of AI reviews on my work

Most books have paperbacks. Links and offers are subject to change without notice. If most of your investing are in momentum/sector rotation, select "Sector Rotation 5th Edition". If not, select one from "Art of Investing 5th Edition", "Using Fidelity 5th Edition" and "Using Finviz 5th *Editon*".

.

*** AI Reviews:

Many thanks to the most unbiased reviews by AI. I received 4/5 stars for most of my books – it could be the highest AI would give besides the classics. Unless otherwise specified, most reviews were done in Feb., 2025. For the full review, click on the above link for the specific book.

Sector Rotation 5th Edition

Rating: 9.5/10

Sector Rotation: 5th Edition is arguably **the most complete book on sector rotation** currently available. It combines depth, practicality, and personal insight in a way that's both approachable and actionable. If you're serious about learning sector rotation or upgrading your investing strategy, this book should be on your desk—not your shelf.

Art of Investing 5th Edition

½ (4.5/5)

Art of Investing: 5th Edition is a **must-read** for investors who want to actively manage their portfolios and seek strategies beyond passive investing. Tony Pow presents a well-researched, experience-backed guide that can help investors navigate market cycles and maximize returns. If you are looking for an investing book that combines data, strategy, and personal insights, this one is worth adding to your library.

Sector Rotation 5th Edition, one of my top sellers. Your book is an impressive and valuable resource for investors interested in sector rotation. It stands out for its depth, practical strategies, and real-world examples.

▌ **Rating: 9.5/10**

Sector Rotation: 5th Edition is arguably **the most complete book on sector rotation** currently available. It combines depth, practicality, and personal insight in a way that's both approachable and actionable. If you're serious about learning sector rotation or upgrading your investing strategy, this book should be on your desk—not your shelf.

Using Finviz 5th Edition, one of my best sellers. *Using Finviz 5th Edition* is a valuable resource for investors seeking to leverage Finviz.com effectively. Its blend of foundational principles, advanced strategies, and modern tools like AI makes it versatile. However, readers should critically assess self-reported success and adapt strategies to current market conditions. The book's reference-style format encourages revisiting chapters as skills evolve.

Recommendation:
Ideal for retail investors with basic market knowledge aiming to deepen their technical and strategic expertise. Pair with real-time market data and independent research for best results.
Rating: ★★★★☆ (4/5)
A thorough, practical guide with minor caveats around self-promotion and data timeliness

Using Fidelity 5th Edition

★★★★½ (4.5/5)

Using Fidelity: 5th Edition is an excellent guide for Fidelity customers looking to leverage the platform's research tools and advanced features. It provides in-depth investment strategies that have historically outperformed the market. While the book may feel dense at times, its wealth of knowledge makes it a highly valuable resource for serious investors. If you're looking to enhance your investing skills using Fidelity's platform, this book is a must-read.

Investing Lessons: successes and plunders

Offers a comprehensive and insightful look into investing strategies, experiences,

Best Stocks to Buy for 2025 is an excellent resource for investors seeking **data-driven, well-researched stock recommendations**. Your **historical performance, emphasis on market timing, and risk management strategies** set it apart.
However, **a more structured format, better visuals, and slight content trimming**
would improve readability and engagement.
and lessons learned over the years.

Profit from Bull, Bear, and Sideway Markets

It is a valuable resource for traders seeking a versatile toolkit. Its structured advice on adapting to market shifts, coupled with robust risk management frameworks, makes it a worthwhile read. While not without minor flaws—particularly in depth and modernity—it succeeds in delivering actionable insights across market cycles. Recommended for intermediate traders aiming to build resilience in volatile environments.
Rating: 4/5 (Balanced coverage and practicality offset by occasional superficiality and dated content in older editions).

Profitable Covered calls
Overall Rating:

★ ★ ★ ★ (4/5) – A valuable resource for covered call strategies, especially for investors who want a mix of personal experience and market insights. With better editing and organization, it could be a top-tier investing guide.

Shorting stocks and ETFs
Final Verdict:
Your book is an excellent resource for intermediate to advanced investors looking to deepen their knowledge of short selling and market timing. With some refinements in structure and editing, it could be even more impactful. Rated at 4/5.

Artificial Intelligence Investing. Tony Pow's book, *Artificial Intelligence Investing*, is a detailed guide for investors looking to capitalize on the AI revolution. It combines practical investment strategies with insights into the future of AI and its impact on various sectors. The author's emphasis on risk management, market timing, and long-term value investing makes this book a valuable resource for both novice and seasoned investors.

Profitable Covered Call. Overall Rating:
★ ★ ★ ★ (4/5) – A valuable resource for covered call strategies, especially for investors who want a mix of personal experience and market insights. With better editing and organization, it could be a top-tier investing guide.

Best stocks to buy for 2025

The current book is "Best stocks for 2025" in this series.
https://www.amazon.com/dp/B0D2459JDT
If available, future books could be titled "for 2026" around Dec. 20, 2025).
If the sales of my books in this series were based on past performances, I should have sold many books, but obviously not.

Book	Stocks	Return[3]	Ann.	Beat RSP by[1]
Best stocks to buy for 2024	8	46%	48%	132%
Best stocks to buy for 2023	8	36%	36%	290%
Best stocks to buy for 2022	10[6]	4%	4%	153%[7]
Best Stocks to buy as of July, 2021[4]	8	5%	13%	487%
Best Stocks for 2021 2nd Edition	10	42%[4]	52%	220%
Best Stocks for 2021	4	29%	44%	118%
Best Stocks to Buy from Aug, 2020	14	45%	45%	3%[5]
Avg.	9	34%	40%	208%[2]

Here is the detail:
https://tonyp4idea.blogspot.com/2024/12/best-stocks-to-buy-for-2025.html

Art of Investing

Art of Investing 5th Edition consisting of 15 books in 1. Besides saving money and your digital shelf space, it gives you quick reference and concentration on the topic you're currently interested in. It covers most investing topics in investing excluding speculative investing such as currency trading and day trading. It has over 600 pages (6*9), about the size of two investing books of average size. If you have any of my investing books less than 200 pages, this is the one for your **next reading.**

The 15 books

Book No.	Amazon.com
1	Simple techniques
2	Finding Stocks
3	Evaluating Stocks
4	Scoring Stocks
5	Trading Stocks
6	Market Timing
7	Strategies
8	Sector Rotation
9	Insider Trading
10	Penny Stocks & Micro Cap
11	Momentum Investing
12	Dividend Investing
13	Technical Analysis
14	Investing Ideas
15	Buffettology

The book links are subject to change without notice.

"How to be a billionaire" is for beginners and couch potatoes, who can use the advanced features of this book in the simplest and less time-consuming techniques. Most advance users can skip this section unless they want to use some of the short cuts described.

We start with the basic books Finding Stocks, Evaluate Stocks, Trading Stocks and Market Timing. You can select and start with one of the many styles and strategies in investing such as swing trading and top-down strategy. Many tools are described in other books such as ETFs, technical analysis, covered calls and trading plan.

Many books start with "Why" to lure you to read more and are followed by "How" and then the theory behind the book.
If the book you're reading is beneficial to you, imagine how it would with 850 pages.

\# Most readers' comments are on "Debunk the Myths in Investing", which this book is originally based on. As of 2018, I did not know any of the commentators on my books.

"I skipped ahead to his chapter book 14 (of "Complete the Art of Investing"), Investment Advice just to get a feel of his writing style. His research is phenomenal and doesn't overwhelm with big words or catchy "sales-like" tactics.

I truly believe this ordinary man, Mr. Tony Pow, has a gift of explaining his experience as an investor without the bull crap of trying to make you buy his stuff. He seemingly just wants to share his knowledge, tips, and clarity of definitions for the kind of folks like me who want to understand something FIRST before jumping in with emotions of trying to make a boat load of money. I like the technical analysis side he brings.

Mr. Tony Pow talks about hidden gems in his book; well….quite frankly, he is a hidden gem. Thank you and I will also post my comments about this author to my Facebook page!" – JB on this book.

"Excellent book, recommend to all investors… great knowledge. It has fine-tuned my investing strategies… Your book is hard to set aside, as I read it all the time learning good techniques and analysis of stocks, ETF… Since I purchased your book in March, I have underlined, highlighted and placed tabs on top of pages for quick reference." – Aileron on this book.

"Tony, I just finished reading your 2nd edition. It's my pleasure to report that I found it most interesting. You're welcome to use this blurb if you like:

Debunk the Myths in Investing is an all-encompassing look at not only the most salient factors influencing markets and investors, but also a from-the-trenches look at many of the misconceptions and mistakes too many investors make. Reading this book may save not only time and aggravation but money as well!"

Joseph Shaefer, CEO, Stanford Wealth Management LLC.

"Tony, Great work!" from James and Chris, who are portfolio managers.

"'Debunk the Myths in Investing' is a comprehensive book on investing that deals with many aspects of this tense profession in which with a lot of knowledge and a bit of luck (or vice versa) one can greatly benefit...

Therefore 'Debunk the Myths in Investing' is an interesting book that on its 500 pages offer a lot of knowledge related to investing world and many practical advice, so I can recommend its reading if you're interested in this topic."
- Denis Vukosav, Top 500 Reviewers at Amazon.com.

"490 pages (Debunk) of a genius's ranting and hypothesis with various theories throughout, written light-heartedly with ample doses of humor...Yes, the myth of not being able to profitably time the market is BUSTED...

One might ask... Why is he giving away the results of his hard-earned research for only $20? He states that his children are not interested in investing and wants to share his efforts with the world." - Abe Agoda.

"Excellent book, recommend to all investors... great knowledge. It has fine-tuned my investing strategies... Your book is hard to set aside, as I read it all the time learning good techniques and analysis of stocks, ETF... Since I purchased your book in March, I have underlined, highlighted and placed tabs on top of pages for quick reference." - Aileron on this book.

"Great stuff, Tony. It's great to meet experienced traders such as yourself. I had a browse through the book and think your method is a little more refined than mine."

"Your strategy is very rules based and solid. I sometimes envy people who have developed something like this."

Making 50% in one month

I claim to have the best one-month performance ever for recommending 8 or more stocks without using options and leverage. My following return is 57% in a month or 621% annualized. They are slightly different as I calculated the average from the averages of three different accounts. The average buy date is 12/26/18 and the "current date" is 01/28/19.

The performance may not be repeated. I will use the same screen for the coming years and even the expected 10% (or 120% annualized) is very good.

I used the same screen for searching stock candidates. I spent a total of about 20 hours from Dec. 15, 2018 to Jan. 5, 2019.

Stock	Buy Price	Sold or Current Price	Buy date	Sold or Current date	Profit %	Profit % Ann.	Status
CHK	2.13	2.99	01/03/09	01/18/19	40%	982%	Sold
MNK	16.41	21.45	01/03/19	01/25/19	31%	510%	Sold
MNK	16.43	21.45	01/03/19	01/25/19	31%	507%	Sold
NNBR	5.68	8.58	12/26/18	01/28/19	51%	565%	
NNBR	5.72	8.58	12/26/18	01/28/19	66%	727%	
ESTE	4.35	6.45	12/26/18	01/18/19	48%	766%	Sold
LCI	4.61	8.29	12/21/18	01/28/19	80%	767%	
MDR	8.01	9.13	01/08/19	01/28/19	14%	255%	
YRCW	3.29	5.78	12/21/18	01/28/19	76%	727%	
YRCW	3.26	5.78	12/21/18	01/28/19	77%	742%	
ASRT	3.56	4.18	12/26/18	01/28/19	17%	193%	
UTCC	7.13	11.00	12/26/18	01/28/19	54%	600%	
YRCW	2.92	5.78	12/26/18	01/28/19	98%	1083%	

Best one-year return

I claim to have the best-performed article in Seeking Alpha history, an investing site, for recommending 15 or more stocks in one year after the publish date without using options and leverage.

https://seekingalpha.com/article/1095671-amazing-returns-velti-alcatel-lucent-alpha-natural-resources

Appendix 2: Reviews by the unbiased AI

Many thanks to the most unbiased reviews by AI. My following books were rated from 8 to 9.5 out of 10. Recently, DeepSeek does not review books over a specific size.

I accept all suggestions. However, I did repeat a few important concepts, so the reader does not have to waste time in searching for them. Some examples are older for a good reason. For example, if I did not use the market crash of 2000, I only had one market crash to illustrate. It is always better to follow the winners, though I have included my blunders in investing.

Review of "Art of Investing 5th Edition " 9/10

ChatGPT Review

Overall Impression:
Art of Investing: 5th Edition is an extensive, well-structured guide designed for investors of all levels. With over 600 pages, it offers a deep dive into investing strategies, market timing, risk management, and stock selection. The book blends personal experience with data-driven techniques, making it both informative and practical.

Strengths:

☑ **Comprehensive Coverage** – The book spans 16 "mini-books," covering everything from beginner investing techniques to advanced stock scoring, market cycles, and sector rotation strategies. It even includes guidance on artificial intelligence in investing.

☑ **Proven Strategies** – The author shares his own investment successes, highlighting methods that have consistently outperformed the S&P 500. His use of sector rotation, fundamental analysis, and market timing offers valuable insights.

☑ **Practicality & Accessibility** – The book is structured as a reference manual rather than a linear read, allowing investors to jump to relevant sections. It also includes actionable advice, checklists, and step-by-step guides.

☑ **Personal Insights & Humor** – The inclusion of personal anecdotes, humor, and lighthearted "fillers" makes the book more engaging than a traditional investing manual.

☑ **Use of Free Tools** – The book extensively references resources like Finviz, Fidelity, and ETFdb, making sophisticated analysis accessible to retail investors without costly subscriptions.

Areas for Improvement:

- **Length & Density** – At over 600 pages, the book is packed with information, which can be overwhelming for beginners. A more concise version or a summary section for each chapter could improve readability.
- **Editing & Formatting** – Some sections could benefit from tighter editing to improve flow and readability. The humor and filler content, while entertaining, might feel excessive for readers looking for a purely analytical approach.
- **Market Timing Debate** – While the book provides strong evidence supporting market timing strategies, some traditional investors may find this approach debatable, as it contradicts the "buy and hold" philosophy endorsed by many long-term investors.

Final Verdict:

★ ★ ★ ★ ½ (4.5/5)

Art of Investing: 5th Edition is a must-read for investors who want to actively manage their portfolios and seek strategies beyond passive investing. Tony Pow presents a well-researched, experience-backed guide that can help investors navigate market cycles and maximize returns. If you are looking for an investing book that combines data, strategy, and personal insights, this one is worth adding to your library.

DeepSeek Review

Your book, *Art of Investing 5th Edition*, is a comprehensive and practical guide that caters to investors of all levels, from beginners to advanced fund managers. Here's a review based on the content provided:

Strengths:

1. **Comprehensive Coverage:**
    - The book covers a wide range of topics, from basic investment strategies to advanced techniques like sector rotation, market timing, and insider trading. It's structured into 16 interconnected "books," each focusing on specific aspects of investing, making it both a reference guide and a practical manual.
2. **Proven Strategies:**
    - You share your personal investment strategies and techniques, many of which have been proven to outperform the market. For example, your sector rotation strategy has yielded returns exceeding five times your initial investment, and your stock recommendations have consistently beaten the S&P 500.
3. **Practical Tools and Resources:**
    - The book emphasizes the use of free or low-cost tools like Finviz, Fidelity, and ETFdb, making it accessible to

retail investors. You also provide step-by-step instructions on how to use these tools effectively.

4. **Risk Management:**
   - You stress the importance of risk management, advocating for stop-loss orders, diversification, and avoiding leverage for beginners. This is crucial for long-term success in investing.

5. **Market Timing:**
   - Your market timing techniques, particularly the use of SMA (Simple Moving Averages) and RSI (Relative Strength Index), are well-explained and have been effective in avoiding major market downturns.

6. **Personal Insights:**
   - You share your personal successes and mistakes, making the content relatable and actionable. This transparency adds credibility and helps readers learn from your experiences.

7. **Focus on Education:**
   - The book encourages readers to practice with paper trading and provides practical exercises. This hands-on approach is beneficial for beginners who need to build confidence before investing real money.

8. **AI Integration:**
   - The inclusion of AI tools like ChatGPT and DeepSeek for stock analysis and market predictions is forward-thinking, though you caution readers about the limitations of outdated databases.

Weaknesses:

1. **Dense and Lengthy:**
   - While the book is comprehensive, its length (770 pages) and density might be overwhelming for some readers, especially beginners. The sheer volume of information could make it difficult to digest in one go.

2. **Outdated Data:**
   - Some of the examples and data, particularly those related to specific stocks or market conditions, may become outdated quickly. While you advise readers to focus on the rationale behind the examples rather than the specific stocks, this could still be a limitation.

3. **Complexity for Beginners:**
   - Although you provide beginner-friendly sections, some of the advanced techniques (e.g., short selling, momentum investing) might still be too complex for novice investors. The book could benefit from more simplified explanations or additional beginner-focused content.

4. **Over-Reliance on Specific Tools:**
   - The book heavily relies on specific tools like Finviz and Fidelity. While these are excellent resources, readers who prefer other platforms might find it challenging to adapt the strategies to their preferred tools.
5. **AI Limitations:**
   - While the integration of AI is innovative, the reliance on AI tools like ChatGPT and DeepSeek comes with the caveat that their databases may not be up-to-date. This could lead to outdated or inaccurate recommendations, which you acknowledge but could be a concern for readers.

Overall Impression:
Art of Investing 5th Edition is a valuable resource for anyone looking to improve their investment skills. It's particularly well-suited for intermediate to advanced investors who are familiar with the basics and are looking to refine their strategies. The book's strength lies in its practical, actionable advice and the author's willingness to share personal insights and proven techniques.

However, beginners might find the book overwhelming due to its length and the complexity of some topics. Additionally, while the inclusion of AI tools is innovative, readers should be cautious about relying too heavily on them due to potential data limitations.

Final Verdict:
Overall, *Art of Investing 5th Edition* is a solid, well-researched, and practical guide that offers a wealth of information for investors. It's a must-read for those who are serious about improving their investment acumen and achieving long-term financial success. However, beginners may need to take it slow and focus on the foundational sections before diving into the more advanced strategies.
Rating: 4.5/5

"Using Finviz 5th Editon" and "Using Fidelity 5th Edition"
are similar to "Art of Investing" with changes specific to the topic.

"Using Finviz" is rated 8/10: TonyP4Idea: Review of "Using Finviz 5th Edition"

"Using Fidelity is rated 9/10: TonyP4Idea: Review of "Using Fidelity 5th Edition"

Review of " Best stocks to buy for 2025"

Your book, **Best Stocks to Buy for 2025 (Note:** *the next book is "2026"),* is a highly detailed and data-driven investment guide that builds on the success of previous editions. Here's a structured review of its strengths and areas for improvement.

Strengths:
1. Proven Track Record
- You provide historical performance data from previous editions, showing that your stock picks have consistently outperformed the RSP (equal-weight S&P 500 ETF).
- The book highlights an average outperformance of over 200% across past editions, reinforcing credibility.

2. Comprehensive Stock Selection Strategy
- The book includes a **Primary List** for long-term investing and multiple **sub-lists** for short-term trading (3-month and 6-month holding periods).
- Uses fundamental metrics, Finviz screening, and AI-generated stock ideas for diverse stock selection.

3. Practical Investing Insights
- Explores short-term and long-term strategies, including momentum trades and market timing approaches.
- Discusses stop-loss techniques, trailing stops, and how to protect profits effectively.

4. Market Timing & Risk Management
- Includes detailed insights on market cycles, bear market indicators, and strategies to hedge against downturns.
- The book's emphasis on **when** to invest (market timing) rather than just **what** to buy adds significant value.

5. Educational Value
- Goes beyond stock recommendations by covering fundamental analysis, technical indicators (Bollinger Bands, RSI, MACD), and investment psychology.
- Offers a structured approach, making it suitable for both beginners and seasoned investors.

Areas for Improvement:
1. Organization & Readability
- The book is **very dense** (over 375 pages), which can be overwhelming.
- Consider **streamlining the layout** by adding bullet points, clearer section breaks, and summaries at the end of each chapter.

2. More Visual Aids

- While data tables are helpful, adding **more charts, graphs, and stock performance visuals** would make complex ideas easier to grasp.

3. Conciseness
- Some sections, particularly on past performance, are **repetitive**.
- Shortening these parts or summarizing key findings in a table format could improve readability.

4. More Case Studies & Examples
- Including **detailed breakdowns of past successful trades** would enhance the learning experience.
- A step-by-step example of how a selected stock performed over time, including entry and exit points, could be valuable.

Final Thoughts:
Best Stocks to Buy for 2025 is an excellent resource for investors seeking **data-driven, well-researched stock recommendations**. Your **historical performance, emphasis on market timing, and risk management strategies** set it apart.

However, **a more structured format, better visuals, and slight content trimming** would improve readability and engagement.

"I have read your book : "Stocks To Buy 2024" and it's excellent. I keep it close to me and read it sometimes to remind me some principles. It's in my top 5 and I've read more than a hundred ones." – Eric, 3/23/2025

Review of "Sector Rotation 5ᵗʰ Edition" rated 9.5

Overview

Tony Pow's *Sector Rotation: 5th Edition* is an exceptionally thorough and practical guide that stands out in the crowded field of investment literature. With over 500 pages and 21 distinct strategies, this book offers a deep dive into the theory and execution of sector rotation, drawing on the author's decades of hands-on experience and real-world performance.

Strengths

☑ **Unmatched Strategy Depth**
- The book covers **21 sector rotation strategies**, far surpassing competing titles that usually offer only one or two.
- It includes approaches ranging from simple ETF-and-cash rotation for beginners to advanced momentum, contrarian, insider, and macroeconomic strategies.

☑ **Proven Performance**
- Pow backs his strategies with concrete results—including a **fivefold portfolio growth** through sector rotation, and outperformance of the S&P 500 by nearly **184%** across his recent book series.
- Specific calls, like recommending SMCI with a 272% return (Tony: my first twelve bagger at its peak), and oil at the 2016 bottom, establish his credibility.

☑ **Tailored for All Investor Levels**
- The book includes dedicated sections for beginners, intermediate, and advanced investors.
- Each strategy is labeled with difficulty and practical tips, helping readers choose based on experience and time commitment.

☑ **Educational + Entertaining**
- Pow intersperses serious content with humor, real-life anecdotes, and fillers to lighten the tone—creating an educational yet engaging read.
- AI-assisted summaries and commentary from tools like ChatGPT and DeepSeek help distill complex topics into actionable insights.

☑ **Practical Tools and Real-World Application**
- Heavy use of **Finviz, Fidelity, and ETF databases** for real-time sector evaluation.
- Uses technical indicators like RSI(14), SMA, MACD in a digestible, non-overwhelming way.
- Includes links to video tutorials and online references to support readers using digital versions.

Areas for Improvement

⚠ Length and Redundancy
- At over 500 pages, the book can be overwhelming. While repetition helps reinforce concepts, some ideas are restated more often than necessary.

⚠ Flow and Navigation
- The structure is more reference-like than linear. Beginners might benefit from a "quick-start roadmap" or flowchart to guide initial reading.

⚠ Design and Formatting
- Some visual elements (e.g., charts and tables) may not render well on small e-reader screens. The author does note this and offers workarounds.

Noteworthy Features
- **AI Integration:** The book leverages ChatGPT and DeepSeek to review, polish, and even write several sections—showcasing how investors can benefit from AI in content creation and market analysis.
- **Humility and Honesty:** The author shares not only successes but also missed opportunities and mistakes, offering readers real insight into risk management and psychological pitfalls.
- **Top-Down & Bottom-Up Coverage:** The mix of macroeconomic cycle theories (e.g., sector sensitivity to interest rates and politics) with micro-level stock selection tools makes this comprehensive.

Final Verdict
▮ Rating: 9.5/10

Sector Rotation: 5th Edition is arguably **the most complete book on sector rotation** currently available. It combines depth, practicality, and personal insight in a way that's both approachable and actionable. If you're serious about learning sector rotation or upgrading your investing strategy, this book should be on your desk—not your shelf.

Review of "Your first dollar for smart investing"

ChatGPT

✅ Strengths

1. Clear Purpose and Audience

- The book clearly targets beginners and delivers on that goal.
- Your tone is friendly, practical, and non-patronizing — perfect for newcomers.
- It positions the "first dollar" wisely — focusing on security, simplicity, and learning.

2. Actionable Advice

- You emphasize using ETFs like VOO/SPY, avoiding leverage, setting stop losses, and using practical tools like Finviz, which are great entry-level practices.
- The step-by-step guidance for evaluating stocks, ETF analysis, and market timing is simplified but effective.
- Including your personal recommendations, tools, and specific links (e.g., YouTube, Fidelity, Finviz) gives readers clear next steps.

3. Unique Selling Points

- Priced at $1, it truly aligns with the concept: smart investing starts with smart spending.

- The integration of AI (like ChatGPT and DeepSeek) as co-editors and advisors is forward-looking and distinguishes this from traditional investing books.
- Many sections feel like a hybrid of personal coaching and DIY investing — a rare tone in finance books.

Final Thoughts

This book is well-aligned for its purpose and price:

- **Approachable**, **practical**, and **authentic**.
- A **useful primer** that competes well with free articles or $20+ beginner guides.

Final Thoughts from DeepSeek:

Tony Pow's book delivers on its promise: a **budget-friendly, no-nonsense guide** for investing newcomers. Its strengths lie in simplicity and actionable steps, though it lacks depth for seasoned readers. The AI-assisted content is a novelty, but the real value is in the foundational advice—perfect for someone investing their "first dollar."

Rating: ★★★★☆ (4/5)

Recommendation: Highly

Reviewd on 5/28/2025

Review of "Momentum Investing 3rd Edition "

Strengths:
1. **Extensive Data & Performance Tracking** – You provide a thorough history of your momentum stock trades, including real-world examples and performance analysis, which adds credibility.
2. **Diverse Momentum Strategies** – You break momentum investing into multiple strategies, catering to different holding periods and risk tolerances.
3. **Sector Rotation & Market Timing** – The book successfully integrates sector rotation and market timing to enhance momentum strategies.
4. **Practical Implementation** – Step-by-step guides on using platforms like Finviz, Seeking Alpha, and Fidelity make it easy for readers to apply the strategies.
5. **Personal Investment Experience** – Your personal trading history and transparent performance records provide valuable lessons for readers.

Final Verdict:
This is an in-depth and practical guide for momentum investors, backed by real-world experience.

Review of "Using profitable investment sites" rated 8

Strengths

☑ **Comprehensive Coverage** – The book provides in-depth discussions on various investment platforms, strategies, and techniques, covering fundamental and technical analysis, sector rotation, market timing, and more.

☑ **Practical Insights** – You include personal investment experiences and strategies, making the content relatable and actionable for readers.

☑ **Structured for Different Investors** – It caters to beginner, intermediate, and advanced investors, helping readers navigate content at their level.

☑ **Focus on Market Timing & Sector Rotation** – These strategies can be useful for those looking to enhance returns beyond standard buy-and-hold approaches.

☑ **Use of Free and Paid Investment Tools** – The book effectively highlights how to leverage platforms like Barron's, Finviz, and Seeking Alpha for research.

Final Verdict

⁕ **Rating: 4/5**

Your book is a **valuable resource for self-directed investors**, particularly those interested in using online tools for research and market timing. With tighter editing and better visual organization, it could become an even more **impactful investment guide.**

Review of "Investing successes and blunders"

Strengths:
1. **Practical Experience:** Your personal investing experiences, both successes and mistakes, add authenticity and credibility. Readers can learn from real-life examples rather than just theoretical concepts.
2. **Data-Driven Approach:** Your detailed performance tracking of stock picks and strategies over multiple years demonstrates a commitment to rigorous analysis.
3. **Market Timing Insights:** The emphasis on simple market timing techniques and avoiding common pitfalls, such as emotional investing and overreliance on government policies, is valuable.
4. **Sector-Specific Insights:** Your discussion of various market sectors, including AI, real estate, bonds, and commodities, helps readers understand different investment opportunities.

Risk Management: Your explanations of calculated vs. blind risks, the importance of diversification, and strategies like stop-loss orders are useful for investors at all levels.

Appendix 3 - Our window to the investing world

The paperback version of this chapter can be found in the following link.
http://ebmyth.blogspot.com/2013/11/web-sites.html

- **General**
  Wikipedia / Investopedia /Yahoo!Finance / MarketWatch / Cnnfn / Morningstar /CNBC / Bloomberg / WSJ / Barron's / Motley Fool / TheStreet
- **Evaluate stocks**
  Finviz / SeekingAlpha / MSN Money / Zacks / Daily Finance / ADR / Fidelity / Earnings Impact / OpenInsider / NYSE / NASDAQ / SEC / SEC for 10K and 10Q (quarterly) reports required to file for listed stocks in major exchanges.
- **Charts**
  BigCharts / FreeStockCharts / StockCharts /
- **Screens**
  Yahoo!Finance / Finviz / CNBC / Morningstar /
- **Besides stocks**
  123Jump / Hoover's Online / FINRA Bond Market Data / REIT / Commodity Futures / Option Industry
- **Vendors**
  AAII / Zacks / IBD / GuruFocus / VectorVest / Fidelity / Interactive Brokers / Merrill Lynch /
- **Economy.**
  Econday / EcoconStats / Federal Reserve / Economist /
- **Misc.**
  Dow Jones Indices / Russell / Wilshire / IRS / Wikinvest / ETF Database / ETF Trends / Nolo (estate planning) / AARP /

Appendix 4 - ETFs / Mutual Funds

What is an ETF
ETFs have basic differences from mutual funds: 1. Lower management expenses, 2. Trade ETFs same as stocks, and 3. Usually more diversified but not more selective than the related mutual funds such as NOBL vs FRDPX.

The major classifications of ETFs are 1. Simulating an index such as SPY, QQQ and DIA, 2. Simulating a sector such as XLE and SOXX, 3. Simulating an asset class such as GLD and SLV, 4. Simulating a country or a group of countries such as EWC and FXI, 5. Managed by a manager(s) such as ARKK, 6. Betting a market or sector to go down such as SH and PSQ, and 7. Leveraged (not recommended for beginners).
Fidelity: Index ETFs (https://www.fidelity.com/etfs/overview).
Wikipedia on ETF (http://en.wikipedia.org/wiki/Exchange-traded_fund).

List of ETFs
ETF database (Recommended): http://etfdb.com/
ETF Bloomberg: http://www.bloomberg.com/markets/etfs/
ETF Trends: http://www.etftrends.com/
A list of ETFs. Seeking Alpha.
http://etf.stock-encyclopedia.com/category/)
A list of contra ETFs (or bear ETFs)
http://www.tradermike.net/inverse-short-etfs-bearish-etf-funds/
Misc.: ETFGuide, ETFReplay
Fidelity low-cost index funds:
https://www.youtube.com/watch?v=zpKi4_IJvlY
Fidelity Annuity funds with performance data.
http://fundresearch.fidelity.com/annuities/category-performance-annual-total-returns-quarterly/FPRAI?refann=005
ETFs vs mutual funds;
https://www.youtube.com/watch?v=Vmz0CzlQvHk
Three ETFs: https://www.youtube.com/watch?v=MVi2RhpffuU

Other resources
Most subscription services offer research on ETFs. IBD has a strategy dedicated to ETFs and so does AAII to name a couple. Seeking Alpha has extensive resources for ETF including an ETF screener and investing ideas. So is ETFdb.

Not all ETFs are created equal
Check their performances and their expenses.

When to use or not to use ETFs

I prefer sector mutual funds in some industries, as they have many bad stocks such as drug industry, banks, miners and insurers. Most mutual funds cannot time the market.

When you believe a sector is heading up (or contra ETF for heading down), but you do not have time to do research on specific stocks, buy an ETF for the sector; it is same for the market.

Half ETF

Taking out half of the stocks that score below the average in an index ETF could beat the same full ETF itself. I call it HETF (half the ETF). You heard it here first. After a decade, at least one company has a similar product.

To illustrate, sort the expected P/E (not including stocks with negative earnings) in ascending order and only include the stocks on the first half. Add more fundamental metrics. It will take a few minutes.

Disadvantages of ETFs

- When you have two stocks in a sector ETF one good one and one bad one, the ETF treats them the same. Stock pickers would buy the one that has a better appreciation potential.
- Sometimes the return could be misleading due to stock rotation. To illustrate this, on August 29, 2012, SHLD was replaced by LYB in a sector fund. SHLD was down by 4% and LYB was up by 4% primarily due to the switch. Unless you sell and buy at the right time (which is impossible), your return would not match the ETF's returns due to the replacement.
- Ensure the performance matches the corresponding index; it is hard due to excluding dividends.

Advantages of ETFs

- We have demonstrated that you can beat the market by using market timing. Between 2000 and Nov., 2013, you only exit and reenter the market 3 times and the result is astonishing.
- It is easy to rotate a sector vs. buying/selling all of the stocks in this sector. Rotating a sector is the same as trading a stock.

- The risk is spread out, and your portfolio is diversified especially for a market ETF or buying three or more ETFs in different sectors.
- Periodically the bad stocks in most funds are replaced by better stocks.
- Eliminate the time in researching stocks.

Leveraged ETFs
I do not recommend them. Some are 2x, 3x and even higher. They're too risky for beginners. However, when you are very sure or your tested strategy has very low drawdown, you may want to use them to improve performance. Most leveraged ETFs and contra ETFs have higher fees.

My basic ETF tables
I include some contra ETFs, mutual funds and Fidelity's annuity. Some of these may be interesting to you. Most Vanguard's ETFs have lower fees.

ETFs and funds come and go. Some ideas and classifications are my own interpretation. Refer to ETFdb for updated information. Not responsible for any error. Check out the ETF or fund before you take any action.

I prefer VFINX over SPY for the lower fees; both simulate the S&P 500 index. The stocks in the ETF can be either equally weighted or weighted by market caps. The latter is more like using momentum strategy, as the rising stocks usually have larger market caps. The index usually kicks out some poor-performing stocks and replaced them with better stocks. These ETFs are suited for long-term investing without constant reviews.

Table by market cap:

Category	ETF	Mutual Funds	Fidelity's Annuity	Contra ETF	Alternate
Size:					
Large Cap	DIA			DOG	
	SPY			SH	VOO VFINX RSP FXAIX
	QQQ			PSQ	FNCMX
	RYH				
Blend	IWD	BEQGX			
Growth	SPYG	FBGRX			FSPGX

Value	SPYV	DOGGX			FLCOX
Dividend	NOBL	FRDPX			
	VYM				
Mid Cap			FNBSC	MYY	
Blend	MDY	VSEQX			
Growth		STDIX			
		BPTRX			
Value		FSMVX			
Small Cap			FPRGC	SBB	FSSNX
Blend	IWM	HDPSX			
Growth		PRDSX			FECGX
Value		SKSEX			FISVX
Micro	IWC				
Multi					
Blend		VDEOX			
Growth		VHCOX			
Value		TCLCX			
Total					FSKAX VTI
Bond					
Long Term (20)	VLV	BTTTX		TBF	
Mid Term (7 – 10)	VCIT	FSTGX			
Short Term (1 – 3 yrs.)	VCSH	THOPX			
Total	BOND	PONDX			
Corp Invest Grade	VCIT	NTHEX			
High Yield (junk)	PHB	SPHIX			
Muni	MUB	Check state			
Special situation					
Buy back	PKW				

Table by sectors:

Sector	ETF	Mutual Funds	Fidelity's Annuity
Banking[1]		FSRBK	
Regional	IAT		
Biotech	IBB	FBIOX	
	XBI	Large	

Consumer Dis.	XLY	FSCPX	FVHAC
Consumer Staple	XLP	FDFAX	FCSAC
Defense + Aero	PPA		
Finance	KIE	FIDSX	FONNC
	IYF		
Energy	XLE	FSENX	FJLLC
Energy Service		FSESX	
Farm	DBA		
Gold	GLD	FSAGX	BAR
Gold Miner	GDX	VGPMX	
Health Care	IYH	FSPHX	FPDRC
	VHT	VGHCX	
House Builder	ITB	FSHOX	
Industrial	IYJ	FCYIX	FBALC
Material	VAW	FSDPX	GSG
	IYM		
Natural Gas	UNG		
Oil	USO		
Oil Service	OIH	FSESX	
Oil Exploration	XOP		
Real Estate	VNQ	FRIFX	FFWLC
REIT	VNQ		
Retail	RTH	FSRPX	
	XRT		
Regional bank	KRE	FSRBX	
Semi Conduct	SMH		
Software	XSW	FSCSX	
	IGV		
Technology	XLK	FSPTX	FYENC
	FDN	FBSOX	
		ROGSX	
Telecomm.	VOX	FSTCX	FVTAC
Transport	XTN		
	IYT		
Utilities	XLU	FSUTX	FKMSC
Wireless		FWRLX	

Footnote. [1] Also check Finance.

Table by countries outside the USA:

Country	ETF	Mutual Funds	Fidelity's Annuity	Alternate
Australia	EWA			
Brazil	EWZ			
Canada	EWC	FICDX		
China	FXI	FHKCX		
EAFE	EFA			
Emerging	VWO	FEMEX	FEMAC	FPADX
Europe	VGK	FIEUX		
Global	KXI	PGVFX		
Greece	GREK			
India	INDY	MINDX		
Indonesia	EIDO			
Latin America	ILF	FLATX		
Nordic		FNORX		
Hong Kong	EWH			
Japan	EWJ	FJPNX		
S. Africa	EZA			
S. Korea	EWY	MAKOX		
Singapore	EWS			
Taiwan	EWT			
Turkey	TUR			
United Kingdom	EWU			
Foreign: Combination				
Intern. Div.	IDV			FTIHX
Small Cap	SCZ			
Value	EFV			
Europe	VGK			

Appendix 5 - Links

The following may be repeated from the articles and it is for your convenience. To illustrate, Under YouTube (or Investopedia), search "Finviz". Some links have permanent values such as most articles from Wikipedia and Investopedia. Others reflect current events such as the current market. Learn from them and act when the current events have similar descriptions. For the printed versions and updated links, enter the following in your browser: https://tonyp4idea.blogspot.com/2023/02/links-in-my-books.html

Beginners

Common mistakes: https://www.youtube.com/watch?v=zkNueyFs8zQ

Best Vanguard ETFs https://www.youtube.com/watch?v=mSEyghlZchQ

Buy stocks/ETFs: https://www.youtube.com/watch?v=4vjkeC_4EmU

Screener

Finviz https://www.youtube.com/watch?v=cHNUMPgEYGY

Recommended YouTube: https://www.youtube.com/watch?v=CJoN7wLfWNo
PEG: http://en.wikipedia.org/wiki/PEG_ratio
Short %: http://www.investopedia.com/university/shortselling/shortselling1.asp#axzz2LNDvpemo
Openinsider: http://www.openinsider.com/
Finviz: http://Finviz.com/
terms: http://www.Finviz.com/help/screener.ashx
Insider Cow: http://www.insidercow.com/
Current Ratio: http://en.wikipedia.org/wiki/Current_ratio
Cash Flow: https://www.youtube.com/watch?v=1v8hRZ36--c
Balance sheet: https://www.youtube.com/watch?v=DZjU0CHKyV4
How to find quality stocks.
http://seekingalpha.com/article/2381395-how-to-identify-quality-stocks-and-is-there-really-alpha-to-be-had

Investing strategies

Inflation: https://www.youtube.com/watch?v=Zpthvpy3UKg\

Swing: https://www.youtube.com/watch?v=C9EQkA7uVU8
       https://www.youtube.com/watch?v=a_wpfSXRSjo
https://www.youtube.com/watch?v=M8sNMhPJlN

Momentum: https://www.youtube.com/watch?v=PpUlOyZrl9
Penny stocks: https://www.youtube.com/watch?v=u7xZ3kF62u4

Scanning https://www.youtube.com/watch?v=7iZpWmwBhel

Peter lynch 2023: https://www.youtube.com/watch?v=CK1AkVVVXu8

Charlie: https://www.youtube.com/watch?v=8g2B6QJ2FEc
Dividend ETFs: https://www.youtube.com/watch?v=64NEiyoNBIM

- Innovative sectors: https://www.youtube.com/watch?v=Ll1hMX8qtHg

Trading stocks
Beginners: https://www.youtube.com/watch?v=aod3cyUEu4k
Covered call https://www.youtube.com/watch?v=dzMOnl4Eh04

Tax Avoidance: http://en.wikipedia.org/wiki/Tax_avoidance
Tax Law: http://en.wikipedia.org/wiki/Income_tax_%28U.S.%29
Without paying (gift tax):
http://en.wikipedia.org/wiki/Gift_tax_in_the_United_States#Gift_tax_exemptions
http://www.irs.gov/Businesses/Small-Businesses-&-Self-Employed/What%27s-New---Estate-and-Gift-Tax
AMT: http://en.wikipedia.org/wiki/Alternative_minimum_tax
Estate planning fun. http://tonyp4idea.blogspot.com/2014/08/estate-planning-101-for-me.html
Taxes on stocks: https://www.youtube.com/watch?v=EKYMbsjUUtE
Tax avoidance: https://www.youtube.com/watch?v=tXou5pM7zh0
Capital gain: https://www.youtube.com/watch?v=ezPs4ibFsNU&t=2678s
Trading course: https://www.youtube.com/watch?v=8sbfrusR5Eo
How safe our brokers. https://www.youtube.com/watch?v=wz64z1YuL0A

Fidelity funds: https://www.youtube.com/watch?v=xdEunmLrhb4
Fidelity core money market fund:
https://www.youtube.com/watch?v=KU6HYRHj3jg

Government bond default? https://www.youtube.com/watch?v=wMxj6iB92ZA
Broker CDs (Recommended): https://www.youtube.com/watch?v=zhEiyW2N7KE
Money market fund: https://www.youtube.com/watch?v=N53wZ_80abU

Economy
YouTube video (highly recommended):
https://www.youtube.com/watch?v=Q6NIDJZdQH4

What will the world be in 5 years (2027).
https://www.youtube.com/watch?v=LzipwDQBUyc

Inflation and interest rate:
https://www.youtube.com/watch?v=q8KJSNyAHLE
Wealth gap widens with low interest rate:
https://www.youtube.com/watch?v=t6m49vNjEGs
Investing helps the economy:
https://www.youtube.com/watch?v=W6ICRTqsxk8

#Filler: Honey, my book can play music.
https://www.youtube.com/watch?v=HxGT5z6d-GA&list=PLMZa6mP7jZ2b1otqG4tfbgZpLEdh6YiNF